FROZEN ASSETS
OR
FORTY YEARS AT
NORTH POLE

Printed in the United States of America

10 9 8 7 6 5 4 3 2 1

LIBRARY OF CONGRESS CATALOGING-IN-PUBLICATION DATA

Lewis, William G.
Frozen Assets : or, Forty years at North Pole
p.   cm.
ISBN 0-87483-335 3 (trade pbk. alk. paper) : $7.95
1. North Pole (Alaska)—Social life and customs—Humor.
I. Title. II. Title: Forty years at North Pole.
F914.N65L49   1993
979.8'7—dc20   93 46474

Cover design: Wendell E. Hall
Typography: Heritage Publishing Co.

This book is printed on archival-quality paper that meets the
guidelines for performance and durability of the Committee on
Production Guidelines for Book Longevity of the
Council on Library Resources.

AUGUST HOUSE, INC.   PUBLISHERS   LITTLE ROCK

FROZEN ASSETS
OR
FORTY YEARS AT NORTH POLE

BILL LEWIS

*This book is dedicated to
all the people who provided me with the memories
enabling me to share them with you.*

FOREWORD

*W*e all sometimes forget what the world was like in the north country just a few short years ago. It is not often that we are blessed with the opportunity to relive the past in such an enjoyable manner as the one Bill offers in his collection of memories.

One is able to see life in the north as an adventure, one day at a time, through the eyes of one that I have both admired and respected for many years. I have known Bill Lewis as long as my memory serves me. I was two years old when my family came to Alaska, which was the same year as Bill and his wife. The world we live in today is not the same one I remember as a youth growing up in North Pole.

Bill's collection of stories brings to mind a time when we did not have to depend on the outside world to entertain us—when life itself depended on how well you were prepared for the next day; a time when the whole town might only have been able to get one car running on a cold January morning.

As you read the stories that are contained in this book, it will perhaps give you insight into life in the early years of a community I have the privilege to call home. It will also perhaps give you a little better understanding of the people that made this community what it is today.

Thank you, Bill, for reminding me of all the colorful people that make up a part of my many memories.

Lute M. Cunningham
Mayor, City of North Pole
March 12, 1993

I've known Bill Lewis since the early 60s when he worked for my father at the University of Alaska Fairbanks Maintenance Shop. I remember a lot of characters, many tricks, stories, practical jokes, and great camaraderie in those days. I'm pleased to find some of them recorded here.

Bill cleared into Local 375 in May 1953 as a Journeyman Building Trades Plumber. When he arrived there was a lot of construction in military-related projects. Ladd Field (now Fort Wainwright) and Eielson Air Force Base were providing construction jobs for a number of contractors. There were also jobs on the DEW (Distant Early Warning) line, Clear Air Force Station, Nike missle sites and an eight-inch fuel pipeline from Haines to Eielson and Ladd, just to name some major ones. Of course manning these jobs brought characters from all over. In the construction industry one gets opportunities to know a wide variety of people. I've enjoyed Bill's colorful tales over the years and I'm glad to see a storyteller such as him compile a collection like this, and I hope there are subsequent issues.

Bill has also served our union in several capacities including a term as vice president, serving on the apprenticeship and examining comittees, and teaching as an apprentice instructor.

Jim Laiti
Local No. 375, Business Agent
March 1993

PART I

*T*his is a compilation of stories I have accumulated over a period of forty years while making a living in Alaska. As I have little or no imagination, and very little creative ability, I have to depend on what I have read or been told by people that I have associated with in the course of living. A large number of my stories have been published in the *Fairbanks Daily News Miner,* where one story a week was printed for more than a year. It would be almost a sin for me not to record in book form these and other stories. It has been my fortune to have been in the right place at the right time, to have been a part of the pioneer building of Alaska in the territorial days and the formative years of Alaska's statehood.

It all started while I was working as a journeyman plumber building an air force base in Del Rio, Texas. A carpenter on the job came to work each day in an old bus that he had made into a motor home. It looked like an old yellow school bus with the only visible alteration being a hundred pound propane tank secured to the back bumper with baling wire. The only distinguishing feature of the bus that interested me was the fact that it had Alaska license plates. I was intrigued and talked to that guy every chance I got. He told me that he traveled to Alaska every summer and worked construction. Then each fall he drove back to the lower forty-eight and worked. He said that the construction season in Alaska started in May and ran until freeze-up (usually in October or November) and that the best time to make the trip was in April.

When April came around, I said, "Hey wife, let's go to Alaska." She, like me, had no idea where Alaska was, but was ready to move. So we hooked up to our house trailer and thirty days, six flats, and four ruined tires later we were in Fairbanks. (Sometime I will write a book about that trip, but it has nothing to do with this narrative.) This all took place in 1953.

HOW I WENT FROM BUCK SERGEANT TO MAJOR IN A COUPLE OF HOURS

*T*he Germans had wiped out the entire area except for my platoon. I found safety for my men in a foxhole where I stood ground at the small entrance camouflaged with underbrush. For two days we stayed hidden until the firing ceased. I heard footsteps approaching. I parted the camouflage and stuck out the barrel on my M-1 rifle.

Someone said, "Don't shoot Roy. It's me, Ike."

I stepped into the open and was greeted by General Eisenhower. "Sergeant Clubb, you have done a good job of saving your men, so come with me Lieutenant Clubb."

I got into his jeep and we drove away. He told me that they were having some trouble securing a hill, and asked me how I would go about taking it. I told him how I would do it.

Ike looked at me and said, "Captain Clubb, that is exactly the way I would do it." We drove back to headquarters and the general said, "Roy, come on into the Officer's Club and I'll buy you a drink. It wouldn't look right for me to be drinking with a company grade officer, so now you are a major."

That is how I went from buck sergeant to major in a couple of hours.

This and many more true and scientific stories are the result of having spent more than thirty years working out of the Plumbers and Fitters Local No. 375 in Fairbanks, Alaska. If you in any way doubt the truthfulness of any of these tales please do not ask for any substantiating evidence.

WILLIAM A. EGAN

*O*nce, while on a business trip to Juneau, the capitol of Alaska, I saw Senator Jalmar Kertula in the lobby of the Barinoff Hotel catching up on what had been happening in the capitol. Jay asked me to come to his apartment that evening for dinner. He said his wife Joyce had some good steaks that she was preparing for us. On the way to his house, I picked up a bottle of brandy that I knew Jay liked. When I got there, his other guests had already arrived. After an enjoyable meal, we settled into one of the most pleasant evenings of my life.

One of the guests told how he became a pilot for Bob Reeves at the time Bob was establishing the famous Reeve Aleutian Airways. He told of learning to fly at the old flying strip in Valdez, Alaska. He had bought an old two-seater plane that had only one seat to accommodate both passengers and was equipped with only one seat belt. One Sunday morning he took his friend out to the field to fly. As he had planned to put the plane through a loop—something he had never done before—he had his friend stay on the ground to act as an observer. He took off, got up to about two thousand feet, and tried to do the loop. But just at the peak of the loop he chickened out and could complete the maneuver. He then flew around and tried it again, with the same results. Finally he made up his mind that he was going to complete the loop or else. As he reached the peak of the loop in the inverted position, the loose seat belt failed to hold him in place. He fell out of the seat and was unable to reach the pedals to control the plane. The aircraft plummeted towards the ground and certain doom. Struggling with all his might, he finally regained control and pulled out of the dive a mere fifty feet off the ground. As luck would have it he was already lined up with the airstrip runway. He landed and taxied to a stop.

Trembling with fright, his friend ran up and said, "You are going to be the best pilot that ever lived."

This said, not knowing how close the pilot had been to sudden death.

Another guest said to the daring pilot, "I bought a furnished house from you and when I moved in I found an airplane propeller under the bed. Where did it come from?"

The pilot replied that he had sold an old airplane to a fellow who didn't pay him, so he went out to the plane, took the prop off, and put it under the bed for safekeeping.

The person who related the flying story was one of the most beloved men of his time. He was William A. Egan, the first governor of Alaska after statehood. He was reelected to the office of governor three times. Those in attendance at that dinner were Bill Egan, his wife Neva, Dr. Les Kleibasidal, Wayne Burkhart, and me.

By his own statement, Bill was the worst pilot that ever flew for Reeve Aleutian Air, but I'll bet that was not a true statement.

APOLLO 11 LAUNCHING

O ne day while I was waiting for a job to materialize, I received a strange looking envelope in the mail. It looked like an invitation to attend a high school graduation and I almost threw it into the wastebasket. Upon closer inspection, I found it to be an invitation to the Apollo 11 launching at Cape Kennedy, Florida. This, of course, was the first moon-walk flight.

Being without a job has its disadvantages as I was without much cash, but I knew that they would have a hard time getting the thing to fly without me, so I decided to go anyway and see it done properly. I am retired from the air force, so I get the chance at space-available seating on air force planes. There were no flights available at Eielson Air Force Base near Fairbanks. I knew Colonel Meta Mills and Colonel Jenny Edwards at Elmendorf Air Force Base Hospital in Anchorage, where Meta was chief nurse. The little police action in Viet Nam was in progress, so hundreds of aircraft were in and out of Elmendorf. Meta and Jenny got me a space-available seat on an air evacuation flight into Andrews Air Force Base, Washington D.C. They let me off at Base Operations the afternoon before the launch was to take place. At 4:30 that afternoon I was still waiting for a flight. I approached a major who was in charge of Base Ops, and asked him if any planes were going to the launch. He pointed to a plane that was parked adjacent to the building and told me to get on board. I told him that I should check with passenger section first, but he said, "No, go get on the plane." So I did. A few minutes later a couple from the passenger section came and got me off the plane, signed me up for that flight, and put me back on that same plane. A short time later, who should get on the plane but Walter J. Hickel, who was at the time Secretary of the Interior for President Nixon. It was, in fact, his plane that I was on. I knew Walter, so we shook hands and he introduced me to a fellow traveling with him.

When we landed at Cape Kennedy, Wally left me stranded, but I

11

managed to get to Base Ops. I asked a major where I could spend the night and he advised me to go to the enlisted men's quarters and find an empty bed. He asked if I was a VIP. I assured him that I wasn't. Then he asked me if I had an invitation; I showed it to him and he said, "You *are* a VIP," and called for a staff car to pick me up. I was chauffeured to the bachelor officer's quarters where I made arrangements for a room. When I asked how I was to get to the launch site the next morning, the clerk told me to be out at the corner at 4:30 A.M. to board the VIP bus.

That next morning it was still dark when I arrived at the bus. There was a man standing by the door dressed in maroon tee shirt and slacks. I thought he was the bus driver and started to speak to him, but another fellow carrying a briefcase looked more important so I asked him about riding the bus. I'm glad I didn't approach the one I thought was the driver because he happened to be Barry Goldwater.

An estimated six million people saw the launch of Apollo 11, so it took an hour and a half to travel the few miles to the launch site. I was riding with General Westmoreland, Barry Goldwater, and a dozen or so high-ranking naval officers that I didn't recognize. I sat with an old fellow who was carrying a 16mm movie camera. He told me that he had recorded every Apollo launch on film since the program started. When we got to the stands, (only five hundred seats for all the VIPs) I helped him carry his movie gear. He asked me to follow him as he knew the best place to view the launch. We sat in the upper part of the stands about twenty feet from Spiro Agnew and Lyndon and Lady Bird Johnson. President Nixon couldn't make it as he had other things to do.

We watched the launch, which was one of the highlights of my lifetime. Oh! I forgot to mention that the old fellow I helped happened to be Ivan Sikorsky, the inventor of the modern helicopter with the back rotor. He had a little trouble changing the film canisters while filming the launch, and said, "I'm going home and invent something better than this." I wouldn't be surprised if he did just that.

When the launch was over, we got back on the bus for the trip to quarters. There was such a traffic jam that it took three hours to get back, so we got into a bull session. Barry Goldwater had been a P51 pilot during World War II and he told about buying a surplus 51 for almost nothing after the war. He was really pleased with it until he flew it and had to pay for the gasoline. He said only Uncle Sam could afford to fly the thing, so he sold it.

My trip home was relatively uneventful. I bought a new 1969 Chevrolet and drove back to Alaska. I still have it twenty-three years later.

Three more payments and it's mine!

CARL BURGER

*C*arl Burger was born in Canada and came to Alaska to work in the cold weather. He was an enormous man and as strong as a bull. Most of the time he was on a job, because of his size and strength, he was on the "bull gang". This is the crew that did all of the heavy work like unloading pipe and bathtubs. He was a bachelor in his late 50s at the time the Haines Pipeline (an eight inch line from Fairbanks to Haines, Alaska a distance of about six hundred miles) was built. Carl didn't go in too strong for soap and water, but he did quite well with booze. He lived in a small shack on south Cushman Street in Fairbanks, right in the take-off pattern of Ladd Field. The air force dumped a fuel tank in the area and wiped out a few houses, so Carl decided to move. His reason was that if they lost another jet and had a chance to pick a spot where it would do the least damage, they would land on his house.

So, Carl got a job on the new pipeline and moved to Haines. The boss told him to unload a shipment of pipe, which he did and reported back to the foreman. They took him off the job for ruining conditions for the other men. Carl had unloaded more pipe by himself in one day than four men had done the day before.

It was beginning to get cold, so Carl went to the store in Haines to get a pair of longjohns. The clerk knew him and said, "Mr. Burger, we have just the thing for you—one hundred percent wool black underwear. It doesn't show the dirt . All you have to do is take it off once or twice a year and polish the buttons."

Carl got a job building a small station in Northway, not far from the Canadian border, some three hundred miles from Fairbanks. The job took two men—Carl and a foreman. They were furnished room and board at the roadhouse, had a panel truck to drive back and forth to work, and kept their own time. Every day at noon they would take off for the creek and fish for greyling. It was a good deal for them all the way around.

After about a month of this, Carl told the foreman he was going to quit. The foreman couldn't understand what could be wrong.

Carl's answer was, "This job is not good. If it was any good, some of those other guys working out of the Hall would have had it."

One of the hands told of hunting ptarmigan (a small grouse) with Carl. He found a covey and shot one. Carl built a small fire, threw the bird on it just long enough to singe all of the feathers off, then picked it up and ate it—guts and all.

He would show up in Fairbanks and make the rounds at night dressed in an expensive suit with a white shirt and tie. You would get the impression that he was a businessman out on the town. The next morning he would show up on the job in his 4-wheel drive Jeep station wagon, ready for a day of heavy, dirty work.

He must have been in his middle seventies when he cleared out of the Local and retired to Canada.

ZEKE WALKER

Z eke and Oris Walker were fitters who had come to Alaska after having worked for Johnny Albright when he was maintenance foreman at a large Coca Cola plant in California.

The subject of tattoos came up on one of the jobs and, for the first time, Zeke admitted that he had a tattoo but was so ashamed of it no one had ever seen it. He went on to explain that he had worked in Los Angeles during the depression, and had saved enough money for a down payment on a Model A Ford. That took most of his money. He had never driven much, so didn't have a driver's license or insurance when he made a mistake and plowed into another car. He knew he was in trouble so he jumped out of his car to try to talk his way out of it. The other driver was a large, young fellow who was not in a very good mood. Zeke noticed that the guy had a tattoo on his arm. In an attempt to take the guy's mind off the crash, he admired the tattoo and said that he would like to have one just like it. This calmed the fellow down, they pulled the cars over to the curb, and Zeke continued to compliment the man on his tattoo.

The fellow finally said, "I got it less than a block from here. Come on and we'll get you one."

That's how it happened.

JIM WALLACE

*J*im Wallace could tell a story that took place twenty years before and describe every part of it in such detail you felt that you were there with him.

On one occasion the gang quit for lunch and agreed that no one would say a word during the lunch break to see if Jim would carry on without interruption.

The story began with Jim living in a small town in the mountains close to Yellowstone National Park. The town had been built in a box canyon and the only way out was via the roadway up the canyon. After giving a thorough description of the town, Jim went on to give an equally detailed account of an avalanche that came down out of the hills and closed off the town from the rest of the world. It didn't seem too serious at first, but after a couple of weeks the townspeople ran out of meat and were threatened with starvation.

Jim happened to be in this town for a hunting trip, so he had his rifle and plenty of ammunition. He noticed that high on a ridge, elk were going into and out of the valley by way of a narrow path. They were forced to travel single file for some fifty or sixty feet. Jim would wait until an elk was at the correct spot and fire. The elk would fall from the cliff, roll down the slope, and the waiting townsmen would butcher it and divide the meat among the residents. This meat was all that kept those folks from starvation for several weeks until a rescue team from outside had repaired the road.

When we picked up our tools to put them away for the night , Jim had still not finished his story. Jim and the foreman were still standing there and the climax had not been reached. We will never know the ending of that one.

LLOYD VANOY

L loyd Vanoy was a welder. Everyone who knew him thought he was the greatest, but he did not have one bit of principle about him. He was so easy going that he didn't care what happened.

The early 1950s in Alaska were tough. Construction workers made good money in the summer but didn't expect to work in the winter. Those who did have jobs were few and far between.

Ray Gossett had a job at the power house at Ladd Field where a new boiler was being added. He rented an old house down on Fourth Avenue and allowed Lloyd and a couple of other hands to stay with him. Ray was the only one in the house with a paycheck, which he brought home every Friday. On one such payday he was tired and hungry, but found nothing in the house to eat. Lloyd volunteered to go to the store for groceries. Ray endorsed his paycheck and gave it to Lloyd. At about 4:00 A.M., Lloyd came home leading a husky sled dog. Ray asked him where the groceries were. Lloyd said that he did get to the store, but someone offered him a great deal on the sled dog; he only had to pay fifty dollars for it. This was more than Ray could stand and he blew his stack. Lloyd looked startled and said, "What are you so mad about? I bought you one too."

Skeets Rodgers, a pipe fitter at Ladd Field, started a little moonlight second-hand car dealership to supplement his regular income. It was located at the corner of Gaffney on Noble Street, and he had a half dozen or so cars for sale. Lloyd stopped by, saw one he liked, and asked if he could try it out. As well as Skeets knew him, it is a wonder he let him have it. The next Skeets heard about his car was from the city police. A patrol car had tried to pull Lloyd over after he had visited too many saloons and was driving erratically. Lloyd decided to outrun them.

This is his account of the incident as given from his jail cell: I thought I could outrun the police, so I headed down south Cushman.

I turned off on a side road out by Rahoi's gravel pit and the next thing I knew, I was in the middle of it with only the top of the car sticking out of the water. I climbed up on top of the car just as the officer drove up.

I said, "Okay, you SOB, if you want me, come and get me."

That's where I made my mistake. The officer dove into the water, swam out to the car, grabbed me and swam back—pulling me underwater all the way.

By the way Skeets, I don't want to buy that car. It doesn't run too good."

Lloyd was driving his girlfriend's new car. She was in the passenger seat when he ran into another car and did extensive damage to the front end of her car and the other car. The impact shook everyone up. Lloyd jumped out of the car, opened the back door, looked into the back seat, and said, "I hope it didn't break my guitar."

Tom Canafax was the business agent for Local No. 375 one winter when Lloyd came in with a job request. Very few of the boys were working that winter and Tom told Lloyd that he didn't have a job for him. Lloyd, with tears in his eyes, let Tom know that he was starving and needed work. There was only one job available—welding galvanized pipe at Point Barrow (four hundred air miles north of Fairbanks). Tom knew that Lloyd would not weld galvanized pipe because it causes toxic fumes which can be fatal. Lloyd assured Tom that he would weld anything to get a job, so he was given a dispatch slip for Point Barrow.

The project supervisor saw Lloyd get off the plane in minus-thirty degree weather in a cowboy hat and boots with a guitar slung over his shoulder. He asked the mechanical supervisor, "Who is that?" and was told it was his new welder.

Lloyd checked in just in time for evening chow. He found his room and some buddies, promptly borrowed twenty dollars from one of them, and went down the hall to a 4-5-6 game (a game played with three dice). When he left the game at 3:00 A.M. he had won thirty-five hundred dollars and paid back the twenty he had borrowed.

The next morning everyone went in to clean up and get ready for work. Lloyd was shaving but did not suit up for work. His foreman came in the door and said, "Let's get to work." Lloyd replied, "You don't think I'm going to weld galvanized pipe, do you?" He got back on the plane and returned to Fairbanks. Needless to say, Canafax wasn't at all happy with him..

A few weeks later, Lloyd decided that he needed some female companionship. He went out to one of the joints on South Cushman and found a gal we'll call "Clare." She had just come up from Oklahoma and was new to her line of work, but invited him up to her room. When he was leaving he said, "How much do I owe you?"

She replied, "Oh, whatever you think it was worth."

Lloyd said, "Good Lord woman, are you trying to rob me? All I got is forty dollars and my wristwatch."

Lloyd was on a bar stool next to his girlfriend when he got into an argument with her. As the argument progressed, he slapped her. For some reason this did not please her at all and she threw a full shot glass of whiskey in Lloyd's face.

He remarked, "Why sweetheart, what did you do that for?"

DALE FINNEY

*O*ne of the brightest young men on the trade in the 1950s was Dale Finny. He said liked living in Alaska because there was only seven months of winter and five months of cold weather. That might be a correct statement for a man from Missoula, Montana.

Bob Terry was his superintendent for years. Bob, till this day, believed that Dale had a criminal background, but would never ask him. Dale had worked for a mechanical contractor who had a repair contract within the walls of the penitentiary at Walla Walla, Washington. The whole crew was locked up for eight hours a day, so when Dale spoke of prison work, Bob assumed he had been a prisoner.

Dale had asked one inmate how long he was in for.

The old fellow replied, "For life."

Dale answered, "That's a long time."

The old fellow said, "Oh, that's not so long. I'm seventy-five now."

One winter, Dale worked at Point Barrow on a natural gas line to the village. After a couple months on the job he wrote his wife and said it might be a good idea if he quit and came home as the Eskimo girls were beginning to look anemic.

He got a quick response from her telling him to come home.

RED FARRIOR

*R*ed Farrior came to Local No. 375 from California in 1950. He bought a fifty-foot house trailer in Los Angeles to move to Alaska. He had never pulled a long trailer so he advertised in the *Los Angeles Times* for an experienced trailer hauler to help him drive to Alaska. A day or so later, a fellow showed up who said he had pulled a trailer from New York to Los Angeles. What he failed to mention was that the trailer he pulled for that distance was a one-wheeler which bolted to the back of his car. This experienced trailer-man turned out to be a plumber and ex-Los Angeles cop named Walter Heim. Red decided to take him on.

They hooked up the trailer, kissed their wives and kids good-bye, and set off for Alaska. Their trials and tribulations on the month long journey are another story and could fill a book. At any rate, when they got to North Pole they bought a few acres just off the Richardson Highway on the Dyke Road and set up housekeeping.

Later, Red drew a homestead by lottery from the U.S. government and built a three-sided log house. They lived in it, but it was never completed. The old pot-burner, gravity-fed oil stove just wouldn't keep the place warm at thirty below. One Christmas Red solved this problem—he bought a twenty-five inch color TV and an electric blanket for each member of the family. They could wrap up in the blanket and watch TV.

Work was slow one winter, but Anchorage had plenty of jobs. Red and a couple of other hands decided to go down there for work. After about a month, Red's wife, Louise, hadn't heard from him. She tried, without success at first, to get hold of him. When she finally linked up with him, she reported that she and the kids were starving as she hadn't received any of his paychecks. Red replied that he couldn't understand why she was in trouble, as he had given her twenty-five dollars when he left for Anchorage the month before.

Red loved his family and in spite of his irresponsibility, they loved him. One summer the hands picked Red up at home and took him to work. It got to be a joke on the job how every Monday morning when the guy stopped to get Red, Louise would stick her head out the door and say, "Red's got what's going around and can't make it today."

One of his kids had disassembled a motorcycle on the front door step. When Red left each morning, he would say, "If that isn't moved by the time I get home, I am going to beat my kid."

Each night the kid would say, "Hi daddy," and Ted would say, "Hi, honey pot," as he stepped over the motorcycle to get into the house.

JOHN ALBRIGHT

*J*ohnny Albright was a plumber who came to Fairbanks by way of working the old Canol Pipeline, the first pipeline in Alaska, built during World War II and operated until the middle 50s. It was a three-inch line from Norman Walls south of Whitehorse to Ladd Field in Fairbanks.

Later on, Johnny bought an established hardware store called Sampson's. It had furnished hardware items for the 1900 gold rush and stocked everything on earth. Access to the floor-to-ceiling shelves was gained by using ladders that ran on tracks. It is operated to this day the same way it was in 1900. Sampson Hardware was located just across the Cushman Street Bridge from downtown Fairbanks. Their prices were usually a little higher in the early days than other places. Someone asked why this was so and Johnny told him that if a customer walked across the Old Cushman Bridge to trade with him, it meant that person had already tried to find what he was looking for at every other store in town.

Johnny was a charter member of Local No. 375. He started a plumbing contracting business which he operated for years. He quit contracting in the early 60s. When asked why he quit, he stated that he decided to give it up when Dan Chandler (owner of Chandler Plumbing and Heating) stopped drinking and started thinking.

Every day Johnny ran what he called his trapline. He walked across the bridge at 9:00 A.M., picked up his mail at the post office, and took it back to his store. By 10:00 A.M. the bars were open. He would stop at the Mecca Bar and have one drink. Then he would catch up on the town happenings at the Cottage Bar while he drank. Next, he would go to the Northward Lodge and, if time permitted, he'd stop in at the Polaris to check in with Elix Miller and crew. Finally, it was off to home for lunch. The next stop after lunch was the Broiler for a drink. Sometimes his little tour changed a bit, however, for some thirty years, this is how he lived.

One winter, someone convinced him that he should make a trip to Samoa. Johnny had no idea where Samoa was, but he knew it would be warm. He had his wife buy two round trip tickets; he was all set for their first trip "outside" in years, and their first trip ever to a foreign country. When they went to board their international flight from Seattle, they were asked for their passports. This was the first time Johnny knew he needed one. Furthermore, he had never heard of a visa. He called an influential friend in Seattle and explained his predicament; the next day he was on his way to Samoa.

They rented a car when they arrived. Johnny said that he almost killed himself and his wife on the first day there—he didn't know that they drove on the wrong side of the road in Samoa.

Johnny wasn't too complimentary about Samoa. He said that the happiest day of his life was when he looked out the airplane window and saw Fairbanks. One of his reasons for not liking Samoa was not being able to do anything for yourself.

To illustrate, he told of his cigarette lighter malfunctioning and running out of fuel. After trying, to no avail, to fix it with his pocketknife, he got into his rental car and drove to a service station where he asked for a small screwdriver and lighter fluid. He was told that they had neither, and that he would have to go to a garage for the screwdriver. After a hassle, he talked the attendant into a few drops of gasoline for his lighter.

That was the end of his travels to far off and exotic places. He said of the Samoa trip that he had never felt so out of place anywhere in his life. He stood on a beautiful beach dressed in a bathing suit with his snow-white body and skinny arms and legs sticking out. Standing nearby was a deeply tanned young man with a perfect body. He vowed that never again would anyone catch him in that condition.

EARL GRANTHOM

*E*arl Granthom was an apprentice in the early 50s. He and his wife lived on one hundred sixty acres which he homesteaded on Rozak Road. In the middle of winter while he was working at the Ladd powerhouse, Earl completed the five-year apprenticeship and was to take the test to become a journeyman. There was a long list of journeymen wanting work. He knew that if he passed his test and turned out as journeyman, he would automatically go to the bottom of the list and another apprentice would take his job; so he decided to fail the test.

One of the questions on the test was: Name three types of traps used in plumbing. The correct answer is: 1) s trap 2) p trap 3) running trap. His answer was: wolf, bear, and beaver. He failed the test, but stayed on the job.

SHORTY MAXWELL

Shorty Maxwell was an old-timer in Alaska in 1953. He saved a little money and invested in a coffee plantation in Costa Rica, and came back to Alaska to work in the summer construction season. While living in Costa Rica, he had acquired a "sleeping dictionary" and was in the process of learning to speak Spanish, but was having some serious trouble trying to master a second, or possibly third, language. He was happily married to an Eskimo woman from Nome and had six kids. He made the mistake of taking her to Seattle one winter where she found a more suitable white man and left him.

One day on the job, one of the hands who spoke a little Spanish, was working with Shorty. While they were loading 3/4-inch pipe onto a pickup they were practicing Spanish. The worker said, *"Un pipa Mas?"*

Shorty understood, but couldn't think of a Spanish answer, so he yelled out, "Hell, no!"

A couple of the boys met the plane one year when Shorty came back from Costa Rica. As they waited while he got his luggage, one of them said, "For a rich plantation owner, it looks like Shorty could afford a little better suitcase." All he had brought along was one cardboard beer box.

LEE RAMERO

*L*ee Ramero's beginnings are not known at this writing, but a chronicle of Local No. 375 would not be complete without at least a mention of his name because of his unique place in the development of Alaska. Some half a dozen members, at one time or another, spent time in reform schools. At least two served time for murder; one, a year and a day for draft evasion during World War II, and many with overnight stays for everything from armed robbery to disorderly conduct.

Lee's background, however, outdid all the rest. He was known as the "hatchet man," and that with some degree of accuracy. He had spent nearly thirty years behind bars for killing his wife, her mother, and her father with a hatchet. This was the result of an explosive temper which had not cooled at all after those thirty years. It makes you wonder who decides a prisoner has paid for his crimes and is suited to be turned loose on society.

Lee was indeed a strange person in the trade. In almost every case, journeymen work in pairs and on each job you are given a working partner. For some reason no one wanted to work with Lee so he, by necessity, always worked alone. On a housing job on Ladd Field, Lee was working for Joe Lane. The general contractor wanted the plumbing roughed in on one end of the building, so he lined out the work for Lee one morning and left for another part of the job.

A couple hours later, Joe returned and found Lee working on the opposite end of the building. Joe also had a temper with a short fuse and upon seeing Lee working on the wrong end of the building, he exploded.

Joe had never seen Lee before, and didn't know his background. He yelled, "I told you to rough in the other end of the building so get your ass down there."

Lee grabbed a ball pein hammer and started at Joe. Joe had a reputation for being a scrapper, but seeing the look in Lee's eyes and the hammer in his hand, he decided that retreat was the better part of valor. He jumped in the company truck and departed Lee's company. Back at the shop he related what had happened. Some of the boys who knew Lee's background filled Joe in on the gruesome details of Lee's past. Needless to say, for the remainder of that job, Lee could work anywhere he cared to, and with very little supervision.

Lee was an extremely quiet man. He did not mix with any of the hands. He worked out of Local No. 375 for three or four years and cleared out. If he made any close friends while he was here, no one seems to be able to recall them. He had a comfortable house in the Highway Parks subdivision that he kept in immaculate condition. With his improvements, to this day it is an attractive place.

JACK PARKS

William Fitzgerald made his appearance in Alaska as a welder, but for years worked as a fitter. In the late 60s he became manager of the 10029 VFW Club. His tales of happenings there could fill a book.

Jack Parks was one of his steady customers. Jack wasn't a vet, but had furnished the property where the club was built and, as a result, he was given an honorary card. It is a good thing Jack hadn't been in the service as it could have extended the war by at least a year had he been on active duty.

Jack was born in Ireland, but came to the states as a child. Fitz tells the story of the time Jack made a trip to Ireland. To prepare for the trip, he borrowed a white shirt and a suit from Gusty, a hat from Frenchy, but couldn't find anyone with shoes big enough so he wore his old work shoes. He didn't go in for soap and water so his complexion was a little dark. He felt that he should have a shave so he went to the barbershop; his face was the only white part of his body after the shave. All of the boys celebrated his take-off so enthusiastically that it took three tries before the airline would let him on the plane. His entire baggage was one small AWOL bag. He was gone three months. When met at the plane on his return, he on the same clothes and was carrying the same small AWOL bag.

Jack lived in a small one-room house on his homestead. One Sunday morning Fitz stopped by his house. Jack, Frenchy, Gusty, and Rattler were all sitting in the sunshine. Just as Fitz stopped, Jack sailed an empty fifth bottle over into the slough and said, "Fitz, you're too late for breakfast."

Jack would show up when Fitz opened in the morning and buy one drink. If someone came in and bought him one he would stay as long as the drinks were free, even if they lasted all day. That, without apparent bad effects. In the winter he would put six half-pint bottles in his parka pocket in the morning. When he reached in and found only one bottle, it was time to start home regardless of the time of day.

In Ireland, he visited the "Blarney" stone and told of how you lay on your back on a steel platform and were shoved forward to kiss the stone for good luck.

Gusty was being teased about being a square head. He said, "I don't know why you call me a square head. My head is just as round as yours and besides, we have more sense than to go around kissing that baloney rock."

AL

*A*l was a welder who was working for Urban Plumbing on a theater building on Ladd Field. Every morning he would complain about his wife. She didn't do anything to suit him and he was beginning to decide to make a change. He made the remark that she was the worst one he had ever had.

This remark couldn't go unchallenged. "How many have you had?" someone queried.

"Six," he replied. "When we were going together, she knew that my hobby was prospecting. Every weekend we would pack our sleeping bags and camping gear, then head out to the creeks, and have a wonderful time. She seemed to really enjoy the outings and could stay up with me all day long. I thought I had finally found the girl of my dreams. She could start a campfire in nothing flat and have a beautiful meal in short order. This went on for several months so we tied the knot. The first week after the ceremony I started to pack up the gear to spend some time in the creeks. I said, ∘Honey, ain't you going to get ready?' She replied, 'You're as crazy as hell if you think I am going to tromp out in that brush anymore.' 'Til this day, I have never been able to talk her into another prospecting trip."

PLUMBERS AND FITTERS PICNIC

*T*he 70s and 80s haven't been able to show character among the plumbers and fitters as well as the 50s and 60s. The annual picnic these past few years did not produce a single good fight. In the past, if a gathering of the membership didn't have at least one good brawl, the affair would have been considered a complete disaster. There was always a softball game between the plumbers and fitters with a case of beer at each base.

At one picnic at Pike's Landing on the Chena River, Jiggs O'Donnel accused Minor Spelhaug of firing him. Minor said, "No Jiggs, I didn't fire you off that job because I wasn't even a foreman on that job. I was just their welder."

The argument continued until Harriet, Minor's wife, walked over to Jiggs and pushed him over backwards.

He got up, brushed himself off, and said, "Minor, I sure thought you fired me."

The annual winter party was held at the old Eagles Hall. Jack Frike stood next to Tex Martendale. Both of them are over six-foot tall. Joe Lane, who weighs one hundred and ten pounds and is five feet tall, walked over to Jack and started throwing punches.

Jack stuck his hand out to hold Joe off and asked, "Joe, what are you doing?"

Joe replied, "I'm fighting you, you SOB."

No one ever knew what Joe was mad about.

That same night, Bob Walker walked from one end of the bar to the other, challenging everyone at the bar to a fight. Luck was with him as no one took him up on his proposition.

AL AND BOB AUSTIN

*T*he Austin brothers, Al and Bob, were plumbers out of God knows where. They were fixtures in Local No. 375 for twenty years. To use an old plumbers cliché, "He was a hell of a good man when he was sober." It was appropriate for both of them. As of this writing, no one has reported seeing them sober.

For years they lived in a small log cabin on Noble Street. It was on the corner across the street from where the Travelers Inn is today. One night, Bob rushed over to his neighbor's house and got him out of bed to call the police. He said that a woman had fallen into the cesspool. The neighbor obliged, and shortly the air was filled with the wail of sirens and the red lights of the police cars. Bob led them to a spot where he heard a woman's voice calling for help. There wasn't even a hole in the ground, and Bob's cabin didn't even have inside plumbing.

At another time they had moved to Slaterville over by a grade school. Al was trying to protect himself from some demon, and shot at it with a .22 rifle. The bullet lodged in the leg of a small girl while she was sitting at her desk in school. This did little to help Al's standing in the community when it made the front page of the *Fairbanks Daily News Miner.*

One day he showed up for work as if nothing had happened, and was surprised to find out that he didn't work there any more. They had removed up his gear and couldn't find it. He made so much noise about them losing his clothes, that they told him if he made a list of the missing wardrobe, they would reimburse him. He made a list starting with a hundred-dollar Stetson hat, two suits of clothes, and enough other gear to fill a steamer trunk. No one had ever seen him in anything but logging boots and a baseball cap.

There was a maintenance plumber on that same job who would be sober in the morning, but by quitting time was barely able to walk. No one was able to catch him drinking on the job. His job was to check the oil circulating pumps and replace belts and bib washers. He carried a hand box with repair tools and oil cans. When they finally caught him drinking on the job, they found that he had filled one of the squirt cans with booze. When he needed a drink, he just squirted it into his mouth.

Al fell on the ice and broke his leg. They took him to St. Joseph's Hospital with the leg dangling. He was already anesthetized with booze, so this cut down on the cost of treatment. They couldn't get Al to sit still to set it properly, so when they removed the cast the leg was healed, but had a thirty-degree angle to it. Al complained with good reason. They had to rebreak it and set it again. This time the results were much better but Al was on crutches for a long, long time. One night after closing time at the Cottage Bar, Al started walking home on his crutches. He fell in the middle of Noble Street and was found by a patrolman in a city police car.

This is Al's description of the events which followed. "The officer asked me my name and address so he could take me home. I had dealings with police before, so they never did get that information from me."

Someone said, "Well, how did you get home?"

Al's reply was, "They never did find out where I lived and I spent the night in jail."

I guess he proved that it doesn't pay to tell the police anything.

One summer Al and Bob hadn't worked much and were broke. It didn't look as if there would be any work for them that winter, so they decided to drive their old Jeep station wagon to the lower forty-eight. There was one problem—no money. This was solved by the membership of Local No. 375 who took up a collection. Enough money was gathered for gas, oil, and bare essentials. A going-away party in semi-formal attire was held at the lodge (the Cottage Bar has held that title for many years) and they departed saying they would never return again. On their way south they stopped in the Buffalo Saloon in Delta Junction, about one hundred miles south of Fairbanks. That's as far as they got that year. In April they were back, signed the out-of-work list, and were raring to go to work.

They finally did leave Alaska for the "Old Country." Rumor says California. Wherever it is or whatever they are doing, you can rest assured that it isn't going dull.

EARL SWEENEY

*E*arl Sweeney started coming to Alaska to work in the late 40s. He lived in California and came up for the summer. When he worked for Boyker in 1953 he was sixty-five years old. At that time Local No. 375 had, as a part of their working agreement, a clause which stated that if a contractor had to have a journeyman after all the local men had gone to work in the spring, they had to pay their air fare from Seattle to Fairbanks. The journeyman had to agree to stay for at least ninety days. If he lasted that long, the contractor had to pay his way back to Seattle.

In 1950, Earl was working on a sewer treatment plant in San Francisco. His boss was Al Campbell. Arnold and Jim Bennett were brothers who worked on the same crew. Their job was coming to an end in May, which is the correct time to come to Alaska and Earl talked them into coming up with him. He had been up the year before and felt sure he wouldn't have trouble finding work again.

They bought airline tickets, landed in Fairbanks, and checked into the hall. They were received in a very shabby fashion. The business agent said that if they had called from Seattle he could have gotten their fare paid and they could have gone straight to work. He added that they were breaking down conditions by showing up on their own, and he was not about to put them to work.

They went back to their camp to talk things over. They had checked out the jobs and found that Urban Plumbing needed men to plumb several thousand feet of utilidor at Eielson Air Force Base. They decided to go back to Seattle. When they got ready to leave, Jim Bennett couldn't be found. He was with some drinking plumber friends at the Cottage Bar, and wasn't available when the plane left for Seattle. Earl, Arnold, and Al left without him.

Earl knew that Mr. Urban was in Fairbanks so he went to Urban's office and told the secretary that Mr. Urban had called him in San Francisco and asked him to come to Alaska and run a crew for him. He also told her that he had a couple of men who wanted to make the trip with him. She knew that they were looking for hands in Alaska and gave them tickets to Fairbanks.

They returned and went to work at Eielson with Sweeney as foreman. This all took three or four days. By the time they got back, Jim Bennett had gone to work.

Earl worked for B.J.L. on a cost plus job on Ladd Field, which is now Fort Wainwright. He reported for work every morning, put on his overalls, put a ten-inch pipe wrench in one hip pocket, a paperback book in the other, and was not seen until quitting time. He had learned a lot on this job. Earl could find more ways to hide out on a job than most people could think of. He would chuck up a piece of pipe in the pipe machine, find a seat with good visibility of the area, and keep close watch. If a boss or anyone he wasn't sure about approached, he would get up, flip on the switch of the threading machine, and start threading the pipe. The moment all was clear, he would switch it off and wait for the next interruption to his rest. It is questionable if any boss ever caught Earl not working.

The restrooms for B.J.L. left a lot to be desired. They were just plain outhouses scattered around the area. The plumbers complained that they were not sanitary. They had a meeting one rainy day and sent the shop steward around to check them out. He came back with this report: "Men, we don't have a leg to stand on. Six laborers were eating their lunch in one of those outhouses."

Earl tells this story about Sonny, his daughter's only child. When the boy was in the second grade, Earl decided it was time to broaden the boy's horizons. The two of them set out on an automobile trip from his home in Palo Alto, California, to Washington D.C. Just before arriving in Salt Lake City, Earl was running low on gas and Sonny was in dire need of a restroom. Earl stopped at a country gas station which didn't have an indoor restroom, but had an old outhouse in the back. It was raining cats and dogs when they stopped, so Sonny made a mad dash for the outhouse. When he got there, he found that it didn't have a roof. Oh well, any old port in a storm. When he got back to the car he was soaking wet.

The rest of the trip was uneventful. They visited the Washington Monument, the Lincoln and Jefferson Memorials, and all the sights in between. When they got home, Sonny's teacher heard about the trip and invited him to make a report to his class. He reported the trip in great detail, expanding to great lengths on the many things he had seen. He finished his description of the whole trip and was about to sit down, when, as an afterthought, he exclaimed, "But if you really want to see something, you should see the shithouses in Salt Lake City."

Earl always stayed in camp. For many years, in order to provide housing, the general contractor or the federal government had to set up camps at the job sites of large construction projects. To this day, it is still done in remote places like Prudhoe Bay, Franklin Bluff, and other sites on the pipeline.

Earl would get a carpenter to build him a stool which he would set in the latrine. After work, for a couple of hours each day, he would cut hair. The money he made in this way was the only money he spent in Alaska. Each payday, he had a stamped, addressed envelope ready to put his endorsed check in and send home. When asked what he heard from his wife, he would say, "Go farther north and send more money."

HOWARD JONES

*H*oward Jones was a Floridian plumber who came to Alaska by way of California. Howard and his wife, Nadine, were very close friends of Larry Spengler and his wife Sophia. Larry took flying lessons, so Howard did too. He finally got his private license and could take Nadine with him on his trips about the state. One weekend they flew to Lake Minchumina for an outing and for one of his cross-country flights. When they started back to Fairbanks, they ran into some bad weather. Howard wasn't worried. He was holding the plane tight on course. About the time he was supposed to see the runway lights, there they were. When he had landed and taxied up to the hangar, he found that he was in Nenana, about sixty-five miles from where he thought he was. It was the only airfield for several hundred miles in any direction. When he got the two of them safely home that was the end of the airplane. He quit flying and hasn't flown since.

Howard was one of the foremen for Thorgaard Mechanical when the Nike sites were built. On one occasion the business agent sent Bud Lindsey out to work for Howard. Bud was known in Local No. 375 as a "Bottle Jockey" (one who always has a bottle close by). Howard knew his habits, and Bud was able to stay only a few days. One morning at about 9:30 A.M., Howard caught him taking a drink and fired him. Bud thought this was quite unfair, so went to the Local Executive Board to plead his case. They, in turn, called Howard to have him explain why he would do such a thing.

The executive board asked Bud to explain what had happened.

Bud said, "I don't know why Howard fired me that morning. When he caught me I was only taking my third drink."

Howard angrily said later to the board, "It wasn't the third drink I saw you take that got you fired; it was the first drink I saw you take."

And that ended the session.

WALT TURNER

W alt Turner was a fitter who made his way to Alaska. For many years he worked "up north" where the men had to stay in camps. He worked on the DEW Line (Distant Early Warning System) at the naval station at Point Barrow. He would set up a 4-5-6 game, hire someone to run it, and watch the money flow in. At the time this was illegal, but since there was no recreation for the men, it was allowed to operate in all of the camps north of Brooks Range. Walt's headquarters were in an eight-foot wide, fifty-foot long trailer behind Sampson Hardware in Fairbanks. In the early 60s Walt had enough of camp life and a little money, so he bought a service station in North Pole, Alaska, a small town thirteen miles south of Fairbanks. He had enough property with the station to set up a twelve-foot wide, sixty-foot long trailer where he and his wife lived. They rented the one at Berry's to some friends. When the 1967 flood put Fairbanks ten feet underwater, Walt's trailer was submerged for several days. The president declared Fairbanks a disaster area, which it was, and the federal government moved in a Small Business Administration office to loan money and help rebuild the city. Walt paid fifteen hundred dollars for his trailer. He applied for a twenty-three thousand dollar, three percent loan to salvage it. They sent an inspector who looked it over and reported back to Walt that they would let him have eleven thousand five hundred dollars, which Walt accepted. He took it down to the credit union, put it in a savings account with seven and one half percent interest and allowed the interest to pay off the loan. Later, much of this money loaned to the people was "forgiven" by the federal government. Walt pulled the old trailer out of his place at North Pole, washed it down good with water from his well, let it dry out for a couple of months, and resold it. Walt knew how to make a dime.

It was such a great sport to watch Walt operate his gas station. His gas was a couple of cents cheaper than in Fairbanks. Walt would say, "Look at those cheap bastards. They will drive twenty-six miles to trade with me to save twenty-five cents." He didn't clean windshields, check oil, or air tires. He said that his place was a gas house not a service station. If someone wanted air or water, Walt would say, "There is the air hose and here is the bucket. There is all the water you want in the pond behind the station." When asked if he had a restroom, he replied, "Yes, there's forty acres behind the station. Help yourself." Needless to say, Walt's regular customers knew better than to ask for those services. He had a large sign made by a professional painter which read, FREE AIR, ONE DOLLAR. The summer tourists liked the sign and took pictures to take home and show how expensive things are in Alaska. Walt never charged anyone for air, but it kept the freeloaders away.

Danny Nichols died, (his life is another story) and one of the hands was going to his funeral. He stopped at Walt's Station and asked him if he wanted to go. Walt said, "No, I don't want to go to his funeral. I just want to remember him as I last saw him—drunk and obnoxious."

The funeral was conducted by a fire-and-brimstone preacher. From the way he yelled, he must have belonged to some branch of the Baptist church. He explained what a loving father Danny was, dedicated to all that was good, a leader of men, and known as a teacher in his trade. He continued by saying that he was highly respected by all who knew him and further expounded on the many accomplishments to his credit.

After the service, Ronnie Powers, one of Danny's closest friends was heard to say, "That must not have been Danny in that box."

Walt's station was located about halfway from town to Eielson Air Force Base. The airmen on base mostly traded with the base gas station because gas was about six cents per gallon cheaper than civilian stations. It would infuriate Walt to have a serviceman pull into his station when the temperature was below zero, roll down the window, and stick out a one-dollar bill for enough gas to get them back to the base station.

BILL ANDERSON

*B*ill Anderson was a fitter from Horseshoe, North Carolina. He came to Alaska via California and the Aleutian Chain. During World War II he was a mechanical superintendent on jobs at Dutch Harbor and Shemia. He arrived in Fairbanks in 1950. Although he had been away from North Carolina for twenty years, he still had his slow southern drawl, and used such sayings as, "He's as useless as tits on bacon rind."

Bill was an avid sportsman. At first frost of the fall 1953 hunting season most of the crew from the Boyker job decided to go hunting. They were going to take a long weekend, go down to the 40 mile country some two hundred fifty miles south of Fairbanks, and hunt caribou. Word had gotten back that thousands of caribou would be crossing the Taylor Highway on their southward migration. The truck driver on the job, Max Anderson, wanted to go with Bill. They started out in Bill's panel truck filled with guns, ammunition, sleeping bags, and a few bottles of Old Taylor. When they arrived where the herd was crossing the highway, they saw hundreds of caribou crossing the roadway and blocking it for over half a mile. Bill stopped the truck behind a couple of cars already parked there. Men were standing by their cars admiring a sight seldom seen. Bill's friend jumped out of the truck with his loaded rifle and started shooting into the herd, missing one man by inches. Bill was dumbfounded. Before he could stop the guy and take away his rifle, he had knocked down two caribou and wounded no telling how many. At that time it was illegal to hunt anything within a half mile of public highway. It was also illegal to kill a cow caribou. Since both cows and bulls have horns, the Braille system is about the only way to tell them apart. When they checked out the dead animals, they found that both were cows.

Bill knew they were in trouble, so he got busy and dressed out the kill. They loaded the meat and started back to Fairbanks, hoping that they would not be picked up by Fish and Wildlife agents. A few miles up the road, they met Chet Jackson and gave their weapons to him, keeping only an old .22 rifle with them. Bill knew that if stopped their guns would be confiscated when it was discovered that they had killed female caribou.

As expected, one of the fellows on the road had turned them in to Fish and Game officials. Just before they got to Delta Junction, one hundred miles south of Fairbanks, they got the red light. The next stop was the magistrate's office in Big Delta. They lost the .22 rifle and put up bond with instructions to appear in court for trial in two weeks. When they appeared in court the magistrate raked Bill over the coals and fined him one hundred fifty dollars. He said, "Mr. Anderson, you are old enough to know better, but I am still going to fine your younger brother seventy-five dollars."

Bill had not fired a shot and was in no way related to the other Anderson, but, Bill later said, "What was I going to do."

Before Bill left on the trip, he and Chet Jackson had gone into the civilian club on Eielson Air Force Base. They were met at the door by a pretty girl selling raffle tickets benefiting air force aid. Bill and Chet bought a dollar ticket each. Bill bet Chet a bottle of whiskey that he would come closer to the winning number than Chet. When Bill got back from the hunting trip, he found that he had won the whiskey and a new Chevrolet. So, as you can see, his luck was not all bad.

Bill was a large man, over six feet tall, and to use his expression, wore a size eighteen shirt and a number two hat. Before the days of blue jeans and tee shirt, you were expected to show up at most gatherings in a suit and tie. Bill claimed that he couldn't wear a suit and tie. One year Bill and his wife, Dee, made a trip around the world and when they returned, Bill was wearing a suit and tie. When asked about it, he explained, "I found out why I could never wear a tie. I had always bought my shirts a size too small."

No one who had made a round-the-world trip ever saw it the way he did. He said that all his life he had been proud of the fact that his mother was English. After seeing how the English were in England, he didn't want anyone to know she was English. He said, "Them buggers can't even talk right. We would go into a restaurant to eat and they couldn't even talk so you could understand them. I'd say, ∘Okay, buddy, you can talk better English than that. Talk so I can understand you.' They could too. Our GIs had been over there for four years, so they could talk English if they wanted to."

About Italy he said, "That place is no good. The city had a crew of men working all the time, trying to make old buildings look old."

On Greece, "They would have a pretty nice country if they would go ahead and put tops on those old buildings standing there."

On Bangkok, "It was so blasted hot there that I didn't even get off the plane, so I can't tell you about it."

On Saigon, "I wanted to see the scummy part of town, so we got a cab and started out. The driver honked his horn all the way at all the people in the streets and almost ran over a couple of dozen. There were so many that if he had killed a few they would never have missed them. When we was kids I thought we was poor. Them people is poor. We weren't."

Bill had two suits tailor-made in Hong Kong, and was amazed that they took his measurements after he selected the material. At 9:00 A.M. the next day they delivered the suits. He bought a small portable radio in Hong Kong and was unhappy the next day in Tokyo to see it was marked, *Made in Japan*.

Bill and Dee toured Australia and New Zealand. The people there were too much like Americans to have impressed Bill Anderson.

Bill enjoyed his Alaska barroom friends, and was asked how he liked the English bars. He stated that he didn't like them at all. His reason is fully understandable. "They don't have any bar stools." Standing at a bar wouldn't be much fun.

One time Bill and Dee had been having fun at the Mecca Bar on Second Avenue, and decided to go home. When they got into the car, a policeman saw Bill and said, "You're not going to drive that car in the shape you're in are you?"

Bill's answer was, "Sure, you can see I'm too drunk to walk."

The policeman was a good guy, so he said, "I'll let you go if you'll let your wife drive."

Bill said nothing could have sobered him up faster because Dee had as much to drink as he had. He let Dee drive down to the corner of Second and Noble where she turned the corner, out of sight of the officer. Bill took over and drove home.

BILL PRICE

*B*ill Price came to Alaska in the early 50s with three of his buddies from Alabama. One of his buddies worked his way up from chain man on a surveying crew to become the general superintendent to Peter Kiewit & Sons of Ohaha, Nebraska. They are one of the world's largest general contracting companies.

Bill was an apprentice working for Boyker Mechanical on Eielson Air Force Base in 1953. The Korean conflict was in progress so security at the base was quite strict. One day after work, Bill Anderson was taking Bill Price and another plumber home. They were stopped at the main gate and asked for their identification. Upon looking at the guard, it was noticeable that he had had a cleft lip repaired. Bill, too, had a cleft palate which was corrected after he came to Alaska.

Bill Anderson and the other plumber whipped out their billfolds and produced their ID cards. Bill Price just sat there as if he didn't hear the request.

After a few minutes, the guard was becoming impatient and yelled at Bill to produce his ID card.

Suddenly Bill grabbed his wallet, pulled out his ID and said, "Does that satisfy you? You harelipped SOB."

Needless to say, Bill Anderson didn't stick around to hear what the guard's answer might be. He shoved the pickup into gear and left.

HOWARD LUKE

*R*ichard Coleman has lived in the Fairbanks area all his life. He married a beautiful Athabascan Indian girl as did Bill Henry and Tom Lincoln. One Sunday Howard Luke was having a potlatch at his mother and father's homestead on the Chena River, about ten miles downstream from Fairbanks. Howard makes extra money by furnishing the atmosphere for the hundreds of tourists who ride Captain Jim Binkley's paddlewheel riverboat. The homestead is the turn-around point on the boat's return trip to Pike's Landing. There, the tourists get off the boat and go to the next tourist attraction.

The Luke homestead is billed as the typical riverside Indian village. Howard's mother would sit in front of the cabin. Fish would be hanging on the rack drying and as many Indians as Howard could talk into hanging around, did. There was no road to the homestead. To get there, you had to travel down Chena Pump Road until you were across from it, then take a boat across the river.

Howard and his friends would be drinking in their favorite bar. When he heard Captain Jim blow the whistle, he would jump into his pickup and drive down ahead of the boat. Thus he was present when the boat stopped to visit the typical Indian village.

This one Sunday, the potlatch was in full swing when Howard heard the whistle. There were ten or twenty couples drinking beer and having a good time. Howard gathered up all the white men, took them out back, and locked them in a tool shed. He didn't want the tourists seeing white men at his Indian village.

Richard laughs about it to this day and wonders what the tourists thought about a village that had over twenty women, a whole tribe of kids, and only one male Indian.

Howard and his friend, Norm Rice, were seated on the bar stools which they had occupied for too long, when they heard a boat whistle. They jumped into the pickup, rushed to the riverbank, got into the boat and swamped it halfway across the river. It was a hot summer day, so when they got to camp, they removed their wet clothing and hung it on some willow branches to dry. They proceeded to lay down, naked, in the flat bottom of the riverboat and go to sleep. Captain Jim had turned around in the river and stopped in front of the camp where the two men were sleeping in plain sight. The passengers were all on the side of the boat to view a typical Indian village. When one old lady saw them, she said, "How picturesque."

Howard Luke's main claim to fame was not due to his ownership in a tourist attraction, but in sled dog racing competition. He won many races in a long career. Howard's partner in the naked episode, Norm Rice, was Indian, but not Alaska Indian. He was a sheet metal worker from Arizona. He said that if you were a young man and wanted to "make out" in an Indian village, all you had to do was walk down the main street with the top of a pint bottle sticking out of your hip pocket.

One of his stories should have been placed on record. He was in a village that didn't have a liquor store, but he had brought along a bottle for just such an emergency. He found a lovely girl for companionship, but had underestimated her capacity. In a short time they were out of booze. They were only about ten miles upstream on the Yukon River from a village that had a bar and a liquor store, so they got into a riverboat and started out. About three miles downstream, they hit a log jam and both were thrown out. Norm barely made it to the shore but the girl and the boat were nowhere in sight. As luck would have it, Norm had gotten to shore on the same side of the river as the village. He raced as fast as he could to report the accident and get help. There were very few trails along the river, so it took him several hours to get to the village. His clothes were in shreds and he was exhausted. The first person he saw in the bar was his girlfriend—she was drunk and hadn't reported him missing. To this day, he doesn't know how she got there or what happened to the boat. Oh well—easy come, easy go.

TED WASHELESKI

*T*ed Washeleski turned out as a plumber in 375. He was a lifetime outdoors man and acquired the nickname of "The Mad Trapper." The Alaska Trappers Association named him "Trapper of the Year" in 1978. This attests to his ability since he was competing for the title with the Indians and Eskimos who have lived off the land for hundreds of years.

When the air force station on Indian Mountain, about two hundred miles from Fairbanks, was being built, Ted worked on the site. There was nothing to do on Sunday, the men's day off. One of the welders would catch a ride down the mountain and explore the area around the river. Gold mining had been carried on in the 30s, but the area was not being worked at that time. This guy would take a shovel and gold pan to prospect the area. To have some fun with the boys, he made some fake gold nuggets out of melted brass welding rod. The next Sunday he salted a spot where he had been panning. The following Sunday he took one of the boys with him and allowed him to discover a pan of these fake nuggets. Of course, the fellow became highly excited. At this point he was sworn to secrecy. The two had an understanding that, in order not to arouse suspicion among the rest of the workers, they would not say any-thing until a normal job layoff occurred. Then, they would go to Fairbanks and register their claims. The next day the fellow packed his gear and caught the first plane to Fairbanks. He missed the howls of laughter from the whole crew, who all had been in on the joke.

Ed Steele, a heavy-duty equipment operator, was on that job. He would gamble at night with an air force sergeant stationed there. One night Ed cleaned the sergeant out of his bankroll, but neither was ready to quit. They decided to play one more hand using their false teeth as a wager. The sergeant won Ed's false teeth and didn't give them back for a couple of weeks.

Bob Zigler was also on that job. There was a very large black bear that grew up in the camp as a harmless pet. The boys all fed Bruno by hand. Many times Bruno proved to be the life of the party with his antics. Bob was a cowboy from Montana, and couldn't resist the temptation to rope old Bruno. So he did just that. By then it was to late to figure out how to get the rope off the neck of a four hundred pound bear that did not seem to enjoy having it there. An air force major was CO of the camp. When he saw Bruno dragging the rope, he issued the following edict. "I don't know who did it, but if that rope isn't off that bear by 1700 hours, whoever did it will be off the job by tomorrow."

Bob got one of his friends to help him. They got a pickup and drove as close as they could to Bruno. Then both of them got into the truck box while some other men fed Bruno apples. Bob was able to get his hand under the rope and get it off, but he found out that you don't cowboy with a real live bear. By the way, Bob kept his job.

One of the laborers on the job had just reported to the camp and been given his room assignment. He was in the process of stacking his gear when he looked around and saw that Bruno was in the room with him. He said, "I never was white before, but I sure was for a few minutes then."

Joe Haig had a picture taken while laying on the ground with Bruno standing over him eating a fish out of his hands. That bear furnished a lot of entertainment for the hands for many years.

Some selfish hunter couldn't stand to be a friend to a tame bear and shot him for his hide.

Bill Lewis as a journeyman plumber in a utilidor at Eielson Air Force Base in the 1960's.

Bill Lewis as Alaska's Director of Agriculture. He retired from this position in 1975.

Bill Lewis was given a commendation letter at a ceremony naming the Plant Material Center Seed Laboratory in his honor in May 1988.

Rope spinning at Will Rogers's Santa Monica ranch in California in 1991.

JED FREEL

Jed Freel served his apprenticeship as a fitter with Local No. 375. He originally came from a small town close to Four Corners, Colorado. Upon his arrival in Fairbanks, being just out of the service and without a job, he hired on as a laborer, working out of the laborers local. His wanting to become a member of the plumbers and fitters showed his dedication to working toward the finer things in life. He was working as a laborer in a utilidor—a ditch dug between all buildings on an air force base to carry all utilities, steam, return water, and sewer. A concrete floor was poured with insert material. When this was done, the ditch was back filled. Finally, the plumbers and fitters installed the pipework. Later, when all work was completed, a crane would set concrete lids on top and cover the tunnel to ground level. The finished tunnel would protect all of the utilities from Alaska's extreme cold. This type of tunnel is in use on military installations all over the state.

To get back on the subject, Jed watched the plumbers show up from their shop at 8:15 and work until 10:00. They laid down their tools, found a comfortable spot, and had a coffee break for at least fifteen minutes. At noon a truck came by and transported them to Universal Food's camp for a hot meal. The truck brought them back after lunch, and they worked until their coffee break at 3:00. The plumbers had pick-up time written into their contract, so at 4:15 they threw their tools into the gang box, and sat down until the truck arrived to pick them up.

When World War II came along Jed was still in high school. As was the case with all of his other friends, he volunteered. This was in 1943, at a time when America was taking a beating in Europe. Jed was put into the infantry and sent to boot camp for six weeks. He then went to a replacement camp for thirty minutes and on to the front lines in France. He took over when some other GI was killed or wounded.

When he first got there, some of the old non-coms would sit down on dead Germans to eat their C-rations. Jed said at first it made him sick to watch that, but after a couple of weeks, he got to where he could do it too.

One night his platoon was to advance across an ice-covered stream. They used a footbridge and after crossing, they deployed to hunt out the Germans. The Germans had set up an ambush and began to mow them down. Jed jumped up and ran into the stream, broke though the ice, plowed to the opposite bank, and managed to get back to his company. The rest of his platoon had tried to re-cross the footbridge and were all killed.

Jed was a large man, 6'3" and close to two hundred pounds. With his size and that kind of experience, it didn't take long for a seventeen-year-old boy to become a man.

Jed said that when he got married, he had a hard time house-breaking his wife. Every time he started to unbuckle his belt, she ran and got into the back seat of his old Model A Ford. Jed had a large family and was a great family man. You could go to his house on Sunday and see Jed in his easy chair, surrounded by his kids and most of the neighborhood kid, watching TV and eating ice cream.

He had lived most of his life outdoors—mostly in the company of men. His language was liberally sprinkled with four-letter words. He could never make a complete sentence without them. Being a true gentleman, when he was in the presence of ladies, he couldn't and didn't say a word. If, for some reason he was forced to speak, it always included at least one cuss word.

Jed later started his own successful insulation business, but continued to work at the plumbing trade.

JACK MORAN

*J*ack Moran was a welder from the midwest who came to Alaska in the 40s. Where he got his training doesn't seem to matter. He had been a professional fighter before the Golden Gloves program became popular. He fought all comers in carnivals, fairs, and any place he could make a few bucks. He did not smoke or drink (which was almost grounds for expulsion from Local No. 375). He worked his heart out for every contractor he worked for and saved his money. His only vice was fast cars. He always had a hot rod, and usually a Lincoln or some other big car, and wasn't afraid to really drive them.

Somehow, Jack ended up with a piece of property on Rabbit Island. At that time it was in the bend of the Chena River, which flows through the middle of Fairbanks. It was considered to be of little value, consisting of a couple of acres on the riverbank, less than a city block from downtown. For some reason, the title was clouded (probably because the property had changed ownership at least a dozen times since Felix Pedro discovered gold in the surrounding hills fifty years before). At the time this didn't bother Jack because the improvements only included two or three one-room shacks, one of which he lives in to this day. As the city grew, the property became more valuable, and he tried to secure a clear title. This resulted in a lawsuit with the city which lasted for over twenty years. A couple of years ago, Jack finally won his case and now owns free and clear property with an estimated value of over one million dollars.

BILL LAITI

*B*ill Laiti came from Minnesota and became a maintenance superintendent for the University of Alaska. As a member of Local No. 375 for years he hired other members to work for the University. His stories of the exploits of some of the college staff could fill several books.

At a Christmas party one year, "Buggy," a short fellow about 5'2" and weighing one hundred eighty-five pounds, drank too much and went on a rampage. He was not in the habit of drinking and three or four of the boys had to take him home. When he got home, he went wild again and threatened to harm his own children. One of his buddies who helped him home was a husky fellow, but knew he couldn't hold Buggy all night. At this point he told his helpers that he had taken judo and with one chop could put Buggy out. He was afraid to do so out of fear of injuring him. His buddy said, "Go ahead and give him your best. It would be better than letting him kill his children."

He let Buggy have it on the back of the neck with all that he had. Buggy looked around at him and said, "Quit your fooling around."

Sam Snyder worked for Bill Laiti. He was a licensed game guide and was learning to weld, so he practiced every chance he got. Like so many other Alaskans, Sam dipped Copenhagen snuff. One day he had the welder hood down over his face and was welding away. He forgot that he had the hood on and let loose with a hefty spit of tobacco juice. He actually spit in his own face.

Ray Gadberry was a young man at the courting age when he worked at the University of Alaska. Bill sent him to check on the sewer treatment plant (the worst smelling place on the face of the earth). Everyone dreaded going down there. Ray didn't come back when he was expected, so Bill went down to check on him. Ray had had a bad night the evening before and Bill found him asleep on the concrete floor in that horrible smelling place.

Bill Willoughby came to work one morning and informed Bill Laiti that he had to quit. He said that he hated to quit, but an emergency had come up. He went on to explain that he had just gotten word that someone had jumped his mining claim down on the Peace River. The Peace River is in Canada, just above Dawson Creek. We had never heard of any gold or silver activity in that neck of the woods.

JIM MARSHALL

*J*im Marshall came to Alaska as an army officer during World War II. He was stationed in the Aleutian Islands where the only Japanese occupation of United States soil took place. After the war he joined a Los Angeles Plumbers Local, then transferred to Local No. 375 in Fairbanks. He served many years as inner guard at union meetings.

Jim tells the story of when he served as scoutmaster for his local Boy Scout troop. One day he took his troop on a hike and camping trip out in the woods not far from home. Late in the afternoon they began to look for a place to camp. They came to an old deserted farmhouse and decided to spend the night. They cooked and ate their meal outside, then went inside, laid out their bedrolls and went to bed. About 9:00 P.M., they heard someone approaching along the road. When Jim got up and looked outside, he saw a group of men in white sheets in front of the house. Being a black man, this sight sent cold chills down his spine, and reminded him of stories he had been told about the Ku Klux Klan.

The leader of the group saw the glow of the campfire in front of the house and shouted, "Who's in there?"

Jim said that he had never been so frightened in all his life, and couldn't think of anything to say but, "Ain't nobody in here but us."

The Klansmen walked to the nearby creek for their meeting and refreshments. The next morning when Jim and the boys got up to cook their breakfast, they found a cardboard box full of soft drinks and food that the Klansmen had left.

Jim said that throughout the years he has gone back to visit some of the members of the old scout troop. One of them always greeted him with, "Ain't nobody here but us."

Jim, in the last few years, has traveled the world as a member of the Bahai faith. One time after work, Jim invited Mark Meyers to his house for dinner. Jim's wife had a good reputation for being able to prepare a tasty meal. Jim was in his regular spot, the easy chair, talking to Mark as his wife cooked dinner. He said, "Mark, come over here and look in the mirror." From where he sat, he could see his wife preparing the meal. She would work away for a while, then sneak a drink out of a mickey bottle (1/2 pint). Jim said that he had watched her do that every night for years, but she never noticed that he knew. Then he mused, "I wonder who she thought carried off all those empties she has thrown out the back door."

Being the first black accepted into Local No. 375 was more difficult for Jim than it was for Willy Mays to break into pro baseball, and a whole lot less profitable. He was a member of the Local for three years before he got his first job. He has never complained. One time, when asked if he would recommend a black for apprentice training in the Local, he said, "No, my young people this day and age don't want to be plumbers because it is hard work. They all want to do something a lot easier."

SOCKEYE'S TALE
IS NO FISH STORY

Sockeye was one of North Pole's most popular cowboys. He was always on hand when the Lion's Club put on one of their rodeos.

One old-timer remembers the horse race Sockeye and Rudy Grassman staged at the rodeo arena on Grace Ford's homestead. The most memorable event Sockeye performed, however, was at the rodeo on Al Remmington's ranch at the Delta Clearwater. It was an event that could have been featured at the National Finals Rodeo in Las Vegas.

Someone talked Sockeye into sitting in a number-two washtub tied to the back of Al Remmington's old milk cow. He was to hold onto the two handles of the tub. With the first jump the cow made out of the chute, Sockeye was under her belly with the cow hopping and kicking the tub and Sockeye. A couple of seconds later, he rose from the dust holding the two tub handles. He received no broken bones, but didn't look anything like the cowboy who started the ride.

I talked to several old-timers who knew Sockeye, but couldn't find anyone who knew his legal name. Finally I called Bob Portman. Portman couldn't remember his name at first. After talking with Jeanne Jones he finally recalled that it was Darrel Thompson.

There is some controversy as to how Darrel got the name "Sockeye". The one that is most acceptable and sounds most like the truth is this one: Years ago he went out with a pretty Indian girl. Someone overheard her tell him, "I like you better than I like sockeye salmon."

WATER'S FINE ...
JUST STRAIN IT A LITTLE

J.C. Bewley was a welder who worked with me on a number of construction jobs in the Fairbanks area. He lived with his family in south Fairbanks on Mary Ann Street. I met him shortly after I arrived in this part of the world, so this happened in the early 1950s.

At that time, the city of Fairbanks had not installed sewer and water systems—everyone had to install their own. Since there were no city ordinances or building codes to govern the builder, it was up to the property owner to do the job in any manner he chose.

The water table in that area was only a few feet below the surface. Most wells were installed by hand driving a two-inch well point until you struck water. In most cases, this was not over forty feet down.

We all did the best we could with what we had to work with. J.C. told me that his heating oil fuel tank was an old wing tank from a wrecked air force plane. He also said that his greenhouse was made using material from G.I. surplus cots that he had bought from the Ladd Field salvage yard. He had built it to fit regular window glass and it looked like a factory-built job.

The sewer system was usually a cesspool installed as far away as possible from your well, but still on your lot. Since most city lots were only 100 feet by 150 feet, your neighbor's cesspool might be closer to your well than your own cesspool. I was having a hard time getting a good well on my place, so I asked J.C. if he had a good well at his place. He said, "Oh yes, Bill, we have excellent water at my house. All you have to do is strain the toilet tissue."

THERE ARE PLENTY OF PLUMBING STORIES TO GO AROUND

*T*he story of J.C. Bewley's drinking water has prompted more comments than any of my other literary efforts. Evolyn Melville said it reminded her of the plight of a few of her friends that lived on Noble Street before the city of Fairbanks extended the sewer system to include their property. A few days after they were hooked up to the new sewer system, their wells went dry.

Bill Henry told about living in Slaterville years ago with his uncle, who had built his cesspool before a house was built on the lot next door. When Vern Nash built his house on that neighboring lot his basement was only about six feet from his uncle's cesspool. The float valve stuck on his uncle's toilet and pumped enough well water to fill the cesspool. It then ran over and filled Vern's basement.

Bill Laiti told me this one about Dr. Geist, the anthropologist, and his old house which he left to the University of Alaska when he died. The University had rented the house to someone who complained that the sewer had stopped working. They sent Doug Jackson down with a cat and a back hoe. He dug another hole and installed a septic tank and leaching field some fifty feet farther from the house. The septic tank worked fine, but the well went dry.

Some years ago, Julius "Corny" Kornfiend, told me this story. In his younger days, Corny was a journeyman electrician and, as a result, had been in almost every house in Fairbanks. In the course of doing some repairs in the basement of one house, he noticed that the homeowner had taken it upon himself to do some repairs to his own plumbing system. Corny found that this guy had attached an automobile inner tube directly from where the toilet came through the floor and then to the sewer outlet. He had not seen anything like that in a plumbing system, and questioned the homeowner about it, mentioning that he didn't think it would pass the plumbing code. The owner said that it was the most efficient job that he ever had.

If it plugged up, all you had to do was go down to the basement and squeeze it out like toothpaste.

SNOWMACHINERS STEER CLEAR OF FORD ABODE

The Fords have been a part of North Pole since long before I arrived in Alaska. The first time I visited the Ford homestead was to purchase seed potatoes from Jim Ford. At that time they had an above-ground potato storage built like the ones in Idaho—above ground, but covered with dirt. Later it caved in because of the excessive weight of a heavy snow load.

Jim worked at Eielson Air Force Base as a refrigeration man. He farmed his homestead, growing hay and potatoes. Jim and Grace have always supported anything that might help in the development of North Pole. I overheard Grace say one time that she never bought anything anywhere else if she could find it in North Pole. The North Pole Lions Club staged their annual rodeo on their homestead for many years.

Since Jim's death in the early 60s, Grace has continued as an avid North Pole supporter and has served on the city council for most of the last three decades.

At one time, while she was serving on the council, someone reported that snowmachiners were violating city ordinance by driving over private property. (Ninety-five percent of people who own snowmobiles don't own enough land to drive them on.) Grace said that she didn't need protection, as she had a 12-gauge shotgun loaded with birdshot, and if anyone came close to her house they could expect a healthy dose of the same. A few days later she heard a snowmobile buzzing her house. She told her fifteen-year-old son to grab the shotgun and let him have it. As the guy came barreling past the house on the snowmachine, her son ran out the door, and blasted away. At the next meeting of the city council, Gene Davis, also a council member, stood up and announced that Grace Ford was as good as her word about shooting trespassers on her property. He did, nevertheless, ask who was going to pay for his goose-down snowmachine suit, which he proceeded to hold up to show the feathers falling out the hole in the back. For many years now, Grace has not been bothered by snowmobilers.

THE LEGACY OF ARMY TOUR: TWO PAIRS OF FATIGUE PANTS

*R*ichard and Juanita Kakac were friends who were often visitors in my home when I lived at 12 mile village and later at 11 1/2 mile Richardson Highway. Later, they helped me file the paperwork for the homestead in North Pole where I still live.

Juanita suffered from arthritis. The doctor told her to move to a dry, hot climate, so when they retired from the military they moved to Bisbee, Arizona where they live at this time. I have visited them several times. If they plan to move to a hotter and drier climate than that, they will have to move to hell!

Richard was the first sergeant of an infantry company at Ladd Field (now Fort Wainwright). Juanita worked at post headquarters as a secretary. In court martial cases she acted as court reporter. She could tell some interesting tales about some of the court cases.

One was a case of a woman accusing a soldier of rape. The woman listed a friend as a character witness. While being questioned by one of the lawyers, the friend was asked to state her occupation. She replied, "I'm a prostitute." Needless to say, after that testimony, the soldier was acquitted.

Richard tells the story about Major General John F. (Blackjack) Ruggles, who was the commanding general of the Yukon Command. While he was reviewing the troops, he made a practice of stopping in front of a soldier and always asking the same question. He would ask, "Young man, what have you gotten out of your tour of duty that you can use in civilian life when you get home?" One soldier replied, "Patience." The one I liked best, however, was the reply, "Two pairs of fatigue pants, sir."

General Ruggles was well respected by those under his command. The welfare of his troops was the most important thing in his life.

RESIDENT RECALLS HISTORIC CHENA LANDING

*R*ecently, Sterling Cox sold a lot from his homestead in North Pole and I was taking him to the law office to sign the paperwork. Steve, eighty-one, is legally blind, but can make out large objects.

At the corner of New Richardson Highway and Airport Road he asked me where we were. I said we were just a block from the Fort Wainwright main gate; he said it was called the "Busby" gate when the government took Mr. Busby's homestead and built Ladd Field before World War II.

As we drove on, Steve pointed to Chena River and said, "You know where Busby's boatlanding is don't you? That's where I saw Will Rogers and Wiley Post land on the Chena River."

I had read, and believed, that they had landed at Harding Lake. Steve said, "No, they landed and were to take off the next day from Busby's Landing. The river made a bend, however, and Wiley couldn't get the loaded plane off the water. Ernie Shermer got a freight outfit and took the load to Harding Lake. Post then flew the empty plane to Harding Lake and they loaded it and took off. That was the last time they were ever seen alive.

"Will and Wiley stayed at the Old Pioneer Hotel. Will came downstairs one night and walked into the bar where old Joe O'Conner was tending. Will bought us all a drink. There were about six of us. I remember I was having a glass of beer, not a bottle. It was twenty-five cents a glass at that time. We had two breweries then—one on First Avenue and one over close to Johnny Albright's hardware store."

Steve signed the legal papers and I took him to Denny's for lunch. He got a free meal because it was his eighty-first birthday.

I know that if all the people who say that they saw Wiley Post and Will Rogers on their last day alive were in one place, it would take a town three of four times the size of Fairbanks to hold them all. I, for one, believe Steve's story.

SPUTNIK PAID MOOSE CREEK BLUFF A VISIT

*W*hen the Nike site was built at Moose Creek in 1957, Thorgaard Plumbing and Heating had the mechanical contract. Bob Terry was the superintendent, Larry Spangler the general foreman, Al Campbell the foreman and the others included J.C. Bewley, Tom Mason, and me. Since I am the only one of this group still living, no one can question this story.

The job was started in the summer of 1957. When the layoffs came in the fall, this small crew was the one that was left to work all winter. On October 4, 1957, the Russians put the first man-made object to circle the globe into orbit. They called it Sputnik. It made a complete orbit of the earth approximately every ninety-six minutes.

One morning J.C. Bewley commented that the *News Miner* said you could see it pass over Fairbanks. Several times that winter we watched it pass over from Moose Creek Bluff. On a clear sunshiny day it was visible to the naked eye.

Many years later, while in Moscow, I was shown the original Sputnik at a science fair—one of those places where all tourists are taken. It seemed strange that they had the original display because it was supposed to self-destruct upon entering the earth's atmosphere. The Russians, however, have been able to do a lot of things we can't. Then again, maybe it wasn't the original, maybe they just said it was to keep the tourists happy.

JACK WAS HEADING HOME ... IN HIS D-8

*J*ack Gustafson lived in a house trailer equipped with a wanigan (to those of you new to Alaska, that is the same as a mud room, lean to, add on, storm porch or storeroom) located just across the railroad track on Laurance Road.

I first met Jack when he and his wife, Marge, operated the M&J Cocktail Lounge next door to Claude Douglass on the Old Richardson Highway. By trade he was, and had been for many years, a heavy-equipment operator. He also claimed the dubious distinction of being the first DWI to be arrested in the Territory of Alaska. He received this honor while driving a D-8 Caterpillar tractor.

Some years ago his boss had a construction job at Blair Lakes, a bombing range some forty miles south of Eielson Air Force Base. On completion of the job, they left a D-8 Cat on the site to wait for freeze-up before bringing it back to North Pole. When the time came to bring it home they went to the Northern Commercial Store on First Avenue and bought enough groceries and booze for the trip. The tractor was hitched to a sled that carried fuel for the trip and was equipped with a doghouse.

Each day of the trip the boss would fly over to see how Jack was progressing. All went well for the first day or so. The Cat tracks were in a straight line heading for North Pole. On about the third day, however, the tracks showed an erratic pattern and went in every direction. The boss landed nearby and asked Jack if he was having any trouble. He replied, "No, this is Sunday, my day off work, so I have been moose hunting all day."

They never told me if the moose hunt was successful, but he did arrive at North Pole with the D-8.

TAKING A "CHANCE ON CLUB 11"

A story in last Wednesday's paper by Terri Grigging-Mckay reminded me of the old Club 11 of years ago. In Terri's story, she describes Club 11 as having, "stark birches anchoring its two front corners." Those birches were transplanted there by Leonard Wright with the aid of a large frontend loader.

John Hemetco built and ran the place for a few years. John was an excellent cook but was more interested in gaming. I started to say gambling, but the way John operated, it was not a gamble.

Every time I went into his place I spent a dollar on a chance to win a twenty-dollar gold piece. If he is still alive, I will wager that same twenty-dollar gold piece is still in his pocket. I understand that he operated almost one whole day before the territorial police shut him down for running a 4-5-6 game. (A game played with three dice that can relieve you of your money faster than craps).

One time John placed an ad in the *Fairbanks Daily News Miner* stating that he was serving a chuck wagon dinner—all you can eat, for $1.49 on Sunday. Even in the 50s this was an unheard-of price. The food was plentiful and good, but only a few people were eating. This, in spite of the fact that there were about fifty cars parked outside. We found out later that most of the guests were downstairs gambling. John didn't last much longer at Club 11.

The last I heard he was running a small hamburger place in Anchorage.

The next time I remember going to Club 11, Gareth Wright was running it but he didn't stay long either. Later, John and Beanie Gregg and their partners bought it. They made it into what it was for more than twenty years—one of the top ten places to eat in Alaska.

For many years Club 11 had the largest seating capacity of any place in the Fairbanks area. Banquets were given for all types of celebrities, governors, senators, and military dignitaries. John served the best prime rib I have ever eaten and Beanie took care of more tables than any waitress I have ever seen. It was always a pleasure to stay and visit with the two of them.

At one time, Beanie had tall pepper mills on each table. One night a group from Eielson Air Force Base was at the club. One of the women in the party called Beanie over, thinking that she was just another waitress. When the lady said, "We don't have a pepper mill on our table, Can we have one?" Beanie quickly snapped back with, "Take that one out of your purse and you will have one." The lady quickly complied.

It was worth the trip to the club just to have a look at the most fabulous decanter collection in this part of the world. I know the new owners, Bill and Judy Splitstoser, will also make you glad you traveled the eleven easy miles out the highway to Club 11.

As a footnote, Club 11's colorful history came to a fiery end in a blaze which gutted the club last spring.

WHEN HORSEBURGER BECOMES MOOSE

*R*udy Grassman was one of Jack Park's foremen at the time Jack had a contract to realign and blacktop Farmer's Loop Road for its first pavement. He was a heavy equipment operator and an amateur cowboy. He was a tall, good-looking man but he had a long neck, so he was called, "the gander." Gander was a horse lover and owned several horses. His favorite was a good mouse-colored roping horse. In some kind of horse wreck, the telling of which would add nothing to the story, the horse broke a leg and had to be put under.

Gander had another buddy who was somewhat of a cowboy. He was the meat cutter at Lindy's College Road Store. They couldn't see a reason for not butchering out the horse and saving the meat, so they cut and wrapped all of it, but found that there was little demand for frozen horse meat other than to feed the dogs.

At that time, Mitt Toss was operating a club called 12 Mile Barn. Competition was keen, including the Shamrock, Pauline's Rainbow Room, Blackie's Bar, the North Star Bar, Let's Go Inn, Moose Creek Lodge, Pete's Place, Bob Casperson's 1500 Club, and the VFW Club, just to name a few. They were all on the Old Richardson Highway, so business was less than prosperous. In light of this and in order to attract business, Mitt gave away free mooseburgers every Sunday afternoon until the horse meat was gone. It is illegal to sell moose meat and to call them horseburgers didn't fly, but mooseburgers went like hotcakes.

One of their friends had gone to school with the man who at the time was mayor of Seattle. They mailed him a six-pound roast from the horse and called it moose meat. They got a letter back from the mayor stating that it was the best he had ever eaten. I don't suppose horse meat would be too bad, especially if, at the time, you didn't know what you were eating.

HE HAD A GOOD SOURCE FOR GLASSES AND DENTURES

Robert Krogstie lived on his homestead on the north slope of Chena Ridge. He was an expert tile setter, so he was hired by the University of Alaska Physical Plant to retile the basement floor and bathroom in Dr. Wood's house on campus.

Robert was a loyal supporter of Governor Bill Egan and always wore a large campaign button on his work clothes. He was devastated when Wally Hickel became governor of Alaska for the first time. When he heard that Governor Hickel was going to be on campus for the June graduation exercises, Krogstie called in and told his boss that the campus wasn't big enough for both him and Hickel, so he wasn't coming into work that day. The powers that be took a dim view of this, feeling that it amounted to insubordination, and fired Krogstie. He didn't contest the firing because it helped his reputation to the extent that he was getting more business than he could handle.

Robert came to the physical plant's Christmas party in a suit, white shirt, and tie. He explained that he did not have to purchase one piece of clothing he was wearing—all he had to do was check the university dump grounds at about the time the students were going home at the end of the semester. They didn't want to pack all of their clothes so they threw them in the dump. His clothes fit him but the tie was a little too loud, so he may have been truthful about it.

Krogstie originally came from Florida and still had ties in that part of the country. He had a box full of eyeglasses, some of which could very well have been classified as antiques. He would let you try them on and if they fit he would give them to you. He said that he had a friend who ran a mortuary where he collected the glasses and passed them on to him. He said this same mortician, every so often, would also send him a shoebox full of dentures. He was always able to find a perfect fit so he had not been out a cent for false teeth in years.

Krogstie has since moved to Florida, so if you have any need for glasses or dentures, you will have to contact him there.

CIGARETTE PROVED PACIFIER FOR INFANT

*T*he fall of 1953 we were working for Bowin, Sealid, Egge, Cummins, and Koon building the eight family residential units at Eielson Air Force Base. Jerry King and Glen Bouton were carpenters and working partners. Glen later became an electrician.

Jerry was living on one hundred sixty acres that he homesteaded on the north side of the Richardson Highway and Boots homesteaded one hundred sixty acres on the south side of the highway. At that time she was living and working at Universal Foods on Eielson Air Force Base. She and Jerry later married and built the Boondox Roadhouse. At least that's the way I remember it. Glen and his family lived on their homestead on Johnson Road, named for Dr. Phil Johnson, not a medical doctor, but an academic doctor.

The job was winding down for the winter and Jerry and Glen were the last two carpenters on the job, so we had coffee breaks together. On one of these occasions, Jerry told a story about a family that had an infant who cried continuously. The parents had taken him to every specialist in the interior with no positive results. Finally they took him to their family doctor. The doctor took him in his arms. He had a cigarette hanging out of the corner of his mouth and when the child got a lung full of smoke he stopped crying. His mother had been a two pack a day smoker and the child had become addicted. So, whenever the child started crying, instead of putting a pacifier in his mouth they let him smoke a cigarette.

We called cigarettes cancer sticks in those days, but almost everyone smoked anyway. No one seemed to mind a mild case of cancer. If Jerry could remember the kid's name and if he is still alive after forty years, it would do a lot to dispel the myth that tobacco is hazardous to your health.

OL' TED KNEW WHAT HE WANTED ALL RIGHT

*T*ed Washeleski came to Alaska in 1948. He was an ardent trapper and outdoors man. He once told me that he had learned about the outdoors from an old trapper friend called Moose John who ran a trap line out of Fairbanks.

He had several line cabins located some five to ten miles apart. He kept them all in perfect repair, and even had a small garden where he grew radishes, cabbage, lettuce, and potatoes. He also kept a supply of wood for winter trapping season.

One winter Ted saw that John was late coming into town. Since he knew where the cabin was he snow-shoed out to check on him. By the time he arrived at the cabin, it was late in the afternoon. He saw no smoke coming out of the chimney and expected to find Moose John in trouble. Sure enough, he found him sitting in his chair in front of the stove—frozen. Apparently he had died of natural causes.

Ted said that it was too late to go back to Fairbanks so he stayed all night in the cabin. He pulled Moose John, chair and all, out of the cabin, built a fire, and spent the night. The next morning he pulled him back into the cabin, and went back to town to report the death.

Ted must have learned what Moose John had to teach him because in 1978 the Interior Trappers Association honored him as "Trapper of the Year."

During the 50s and 60s very few of the building-trades people worked year round. Most of us loafed all winter. One year Peter Keiwit had a contract to build an Air Force installation on Indian Mountain. Ted was lucky enough to be on the job.

In those days women were not allowed to work on the isolated sites so the maid work was done by the "bull cook" who was usually an older man. Ted worked for several months but in the middle of the winter he quit and came to town.

When I saw him I asked him why he quit the only job going. He said, "Bill, that's no place for a sex maniac to be."

He now lives with his wife, Larain, at 9 mile Chena Hot Springs Road. When I told her the story she said, "That's my Ted."

FOWLER GAVE A GOOD LOOK AT THE EARLY DAYS

*F*or several years one of the best places to eat in the Fairbanks area was Fowler's. It was located on Farmers Loop Road somewhere in the neighborhood of the Country Club Golf Course. It was operated by Mrs. Fowler, Jimmy Desmond's mother. He is the owner and operator of Western Mechanical on Van Horn Road. If my memory serves me right, the restaurant was on Charles Fowler's homestead and in his log house.

We often drove out from North Pole for Sunday afternoon dinner. One Sunday when a group of us stopped in, Mrs. Fowler informed me that Mr. Fowler was upstairs, not feeling too well, and would like to have some company. We went up and spent several hours with him.

He had come to Alaska as a young man during the '98 gold rush. He told me of coming up over Chilkoot Pass and working his way to Dawson City and on to Fairbanks. He said in those days you didn't have to have any money to live.

Many people were moving all of their possessions and personal gear to the gold fields, so if you were young and strong, you could earn your keep by helping others. He said you could go anywhere in Alaska on foot. All of the roads and trails were well traveled and a roadhouse was located about every ten miles.

If you were following a river it was no trouble to catch a ride with someone if you were willing to work. The steamships used wood for fuel, so wood had to be cut and there was always loading and unloading to be done.

Mr. Fowler gave me a list of all you needed to be on your own in Alaska: a .22 rifle, a fish hook and line, matches, a small amount of salt, and a package of tea (never coffee because it took up too much space).

This took place in 1957 or 1958 and was one of the most

enjoyable afternoons I ever spent. I only wish that I had gone back more often to visit Charley as he died shortly after that one visit.

MORE CHINCHILLAS, AND HOLD THE TACO SAUCE

*T*he Moose Creek Lodge was the meeting place for folks who lived in the vicinity of Eielson Air Force Base. Some of the regulars thirty years ago included Joe Oats, who owned a fish wheel on the Little Salcha River; Pete Cardero, who later owned and operated Pete's Place; August Dehls (Alias Rattler); Jack Parks, who owned the 16 Mile Garage; Ed Steele, who worked for Peter Kiewit; and "Frenchie" Beauchane, who's first name was Clarence. The group included military people from private to general.

At that time, the lodge was operated by Tom and Jeanne Jones. For years it was the stopping place for Fairbanksans on a trip down the Richardson Highway. The establishment had moved several times. Originally, it had been located near the mouths of Moose Creek and the Tanana River, but had to be relocated when the Moose Creek dike was built. It was moved to a site close to the main gate of Eielson Air Force Base. That was the location of the club when Tom and Jeanne first bought it. Sometime later, it was found to be on U.S. government property, so it had to be moved yet another time. The only privately-owned land available in that area at the time was on Bob Casperson's homestead. Tom and Jeanne signed a ten-year lease and built a new log building. When the ten years were up, Casperson wouldn't extend the lease so they moved across the highway and built another club that they operated for several years. Later, they moved again to the present location on Bob Portman's homestead. Sally Portman and Jeanne Jones are sisters.

Jeanne Jones was an excellent cook. In those days Mexican food was almost unheard of in the "frozen north" so Jeanne added it to her menu. She served tacos, enchiladas, tamales, and chili.

Glen and Lorene Elum were regular customers at Moose Creek Lodge. They came in for dinner one evening and Glen ordered Mexican food. Jeanne asked him what kind of Mexican food he wanted and he said, "Just bring me a plate of chinchillas like I had the last time I was here."

HEART ATTACK BRINGS ONE TO REALITY—SORT OF

*I*f you are planning a heart attack in the near future, you would do well to take my advice and repel the temptation to do so. If you decide to go ahead and have one anyway, it would be good if you did it the way I did.

First, you should pick a place close to a hospital that has an intensive care facility. I chose Fairbanks Memorial Hospital. Next, you should drive yourself to the hospital and park illegally near the door. Then, stagger inside and ask the first person you see for a nitroglycerin pill. That will immediately alert them to the fact that you are having chest pain.

Before you know it you will be on your back with an IV in each arm, suction cups stuck all over your chest, and an EKG machine kicking out reams of paperwork. While all this is going on, you should be ready to sign a handful of papers giving permission for the doctors to do all the things they have already done to you. Oh yeah, I forgot to mention, in the midst of all this they are drawing blood. I thought drawing blood went out in the middle ages but it is still done at least once a day in hospitals the world over.

I don't remember at what point in this procedure Dr. Burger took over. He went to work on me and may well have been responsible for my being able to write this book. He determined that my heart was not working properly and decided that I needed a pacemaker. That's when he cut a hole in my shoulder, inserted a catheter into the vein going to the heart, shoved the pacemaker into the catheter, and sewed me up. He did all of this while we were cracking jokes to each other. They took the pacemaker out when it became clear that I was not going to "buy the farm."

Next, they wheeled me up to the intensive care unit. I spent five days there under the twenty-four-hour care of a couple of the most dedicated and caring nurses that a sick, old man could have been lucky enough to draw. They were Diane Mitchell, Teri Kiss, and a third nurse who attended to me in their absence whose name I don't remember. The last nurse had only been in Alaska for three months. She lives in the Rosie Creek area with her husband and four children and says she's in love with Alaska.

After five days I was transferred to Bassett Army Community Hospital where I spent another nine days. Finally, they sent me home with instructions on how to avoid a recurrence of this problem. Drs. Gendren and Wentland gave me eating-habit instructions. I can eat all the eggs I want as long as I don't eat more than one a week and even one grain of salt is too much. My diet from that day forward has consisted of all I want to eat of everything I don't like. I plan to keep following all instructions.

One doctor told me that if I followed their instructions there was no reason why I couldn't reach the age of seventy-five. It didn't thrill me since I was already almost seventy-eight.

One old fellow I worked with years ago said he knew that the good Lord put all of us on the earth for a reason. He said that he would put off finding the reason for as long as possible—I'm doing the same.

PAUL SLEPPY WAS CAREFUL OF WHAT HE WORE

*I*f you have lived in North Pole long, you have probably noticed a little old man at Super Valu Mall sitting on the bench at the corner of Super Valu's liquor store. He usually has a Diamond Willow cane in one hand and a milk carton in the other. He has lived in this neck of the woods since the early 50s. When he was younger he was an accomplished golfer and in the 1930s he won several tournaments around the Long Beach, California area. Several years ago when he was sixty-two, he went to Anchorage for a tournament. When I saw him after that trip I asked how he came out. He said, "Not bad. Out of a field of twenty-two I came in thirty-fifth." His name is Paul Sleppy.

Back in 1955 Sleppy worked on Eielson Air Force Base. A couple of his working buddies were Red Farrior and Ronnie Powers. Emmett Parson, who worked for many years for Nordun Construction, could sell anything to anyone. He came on the job selling tailor-made suits. In those days you could buy a Botany 500 for fifty dollars, but it's hard to sell a suit to a construction worker. Knowing that his customers were good drinking hands Parson's selling point was that his suits were "puke proof." All you had to do was wipe them off with your hand.

The selling point was acceptable to Red and Ronnie, but Paul resisted the temptation even though he could have used one from time to time.

TIME TO PASS ON THE PORK, THANK YOU

So many requests have come for me to write another Paul Sleppy story that I am going to oblige, even though it might well end a friendship of almost forty years. Being a dedicated North Pole news reporter, I am going to report this news though it is now several years old and will likely end my relationship with the *News Miner*.

Bobby Wilson was staying at Paul's house one summer when they decided to buy a pig. They wanted to fatten it, then butcher it in the fall so they would have meat for the winter. They bought a little pig from Don McKee and built a huge pen in Sleppy's back yard. Everything went well that summer and the little pig grew into a very large pig.

Paul had gone to town one day and when he returned the pig was nowhere to be seen. On further investigation he found that the pig had fallen into his cesspool. There was a hole in the top through which the cesspool was pumped out when it got too full. The pig was thrashing around in the water. By the time they erected a tripod and were able to remove the pig from the mess, it had passed away. They decided to butcher it at once.

Bob and Slep, under the circumstances, didn't want to save the meat for winter use. Since they had a number of social obligations to be repaid, they decided to have a Hawaiian luau. They invited a number of guests and barbecued the pig. Their imitation beach party was a howling success.

The reason I have been so long in reporting this social event was to see how many of those guests had to go to the hospital. There were however, no reports of ill effects from this outing.

Today I saw Chuck Leslie at McDonalds. He said he remembered the pig feed that Bob and Paul gave. He had been invited, but for some reason had been unable to attend. When I told him how the pig had met his untimely demise, he seemed thankful he had missed the occasion.

AWOL SOLDIER HIKED EIGHT HUNDRED MILES FROM NOME TO VALDEZ

*H*arry Bowers worked out of the Ironworkers Local union. He was one of the best and ran most of the jobs he worked on. He lived in Highway Park within walking distance of Blackie's Bar and he told me this story sometime in the 1960s.

During World War I, Harry served in France and Germany. When he was shipped back to the states, still in his teens, he was without a trade; therefore, job prospects were slim. A recruiting sergeant promised him a promotion and his choice of any stateside station he wanted if he would reenlist for a four-year hitch.

Three days later he was a private on his way to Nome, Alaska. There was a small company stationed there to protect the Signal Corps from the gold miners or vice versa. Harry's duty was so boring that he hated every minute of it. He and his buddy decided to go AWOL (Absent Without Leave).

They walked from Nome to Valdez.

This is a good eight-hundred mile trip as the crow flies. It now seems like an impossible task, but they followed the old Signal Corps telegraph line, the only link from Nome to the outside world at the time.

About every twenty or thirty miles along the line was a maintenance camp of four or five people who kept the telegraph line in working order. These men, in most cases, were not satisfied with their isolated life and were in sympathy with Harry and his buddy. Besides, they were pleased to see strange faces. They took this dynamic duo in, fed them for a few days, gave them directions to the next camp, and sent them on their way.

The journey took several months to complete. Once in Valdez, they decided to go south until they found a warm place and then turn themselves into the army. At Valdez, they stowed away on the old *Alaska Steamship*. At the end of the voyage they worked their way to Yuma, Arizona, where they turned themselves in at a small military installation. The army forgave them by giving them six months in the stockade and a dishonorable discharge.

Despite his ordeal, Harry couldn't wait to return to Alaska. He came back up, made his home, and became one of the most respected men in his trade. As an iron worker, he was accustomed to walking iron beams high in the air. Ironically, he died in a freak accident while working on a construction job in the early 1970s. He fell off a six-foot ladder to a concrete floor and was killed.

ORIE GIVES UP DREAM OF FLYING

Orie Whittle lived in a house he built on Davidson Road about a block south of Wescott Gardens. His dad, Bert Whittle, who was superintendent for Peter Kiewit for many years, told me the following story about Orie.

During World War II, Orie couldn't talk about anything but owning and flying an airplane. Right after the war was over, Bert told Orie that they could catch the train from where they lived, close to Fort Leonard Wood, Missouri, to Denver, where he would buy his son an airplane.

They traveled to Denver and looked at all the second-hand planes for sale. They found a nice little airplane and agreed on a price. As Bert looked the plane over, he noticed that the propeller had some splinters. He told the guy that he would take the plane if he put a new prop on it. The salesman agreed and the deal was closed with the understanding that the plane would be delivered to Missouri.

Of course, Orie wanted to fly back in his "new" plane. His father agreed as it cut down on the cost of train fare back home. The pilot and Orie took off from Denver and almost made it to Orie's home. The mechanic who replaced the propeller hadn't tightened the bolts on the new prop and it flew off. They were forced to make a dead-stick landing. The pilot looked down and saw a beautiful ten-acre field that was perfect for a landing. What he didn't know was that a couple of days earlier, the farmer had put a hog fence across the middle of the field.

Bert said, "The crash didn't hurt either one of them, but it probably saved me a lot of money. It wrecked the plane and Orie has never said anything more about flying."

EVIDENCE OF "HORIZONTAL HADDEN'S" HANDIWORK SURVIVES

Some folks may remember Hadden Davis, who owned and operated the Davis Log Mill at 6 mile Old Richardson Highway. His nickname was "Horizontal Hadden" because when you went to see him about some work he was always lying on the couch watching TV.

He built a mill that made turned house logs. Thirty years later his homemade mill is still turning out beautiful milled house logs. I believe that he made most of the lathes and coping machines himself. He furnished the logs for the Eielson area Grange Hall in North Pole and he and his wife attended a lot of meetings there even though they belonged to the Two Rivers Grange.

They came to one of our meetings when Hadden's leg was in a cast. It isn't a good idea to even ask a person why he is wearing a cast because it will usually end up to be a long story.

It seems that Hadden was moose hunting and shot this large bull moose, but didn't make a perfect shot. The moose began to go around in smaller and smaller circles refusing to fall, so Hadden walked up to the moose to push it down. The moose made a turn and fell over dead—on Hadden's right leg. I didn't stay to hear how he got out from under the moose, but he must have, as he was at the meeting.

It isn't a good idea to start moose stories either. There seems to be no end to them. I'm sure that if you've been in Alaska for more than two days you have heard a few.

Tankersly lived in Highway Park, part of the old Finnel homestead. He was a sergeant stationed at "A" battery Nike site at Moose Creek Bluff. He was a cook and an avid outdoors man to hear him tell it. Actually, you seldom saw him outdoors. Moose season came along and he hunted everyday with no success.

He woke up one night and went to the bathroom without turning on the light. Out the bathroom window, he saw a big bull moose standing not thirty feet away. Tankersly tiptoed in and got his 30.06 rifle and fired a shot through the unopened window. He said his wife turned a back somersault out of bed, thinking he had committed suicide.

She said, "Tankersly, what are you doing?"

He said, "What does it look like I'm doing? I'm moose hunting." He missed the moose.

Darrel McBerney told this one: A friend of his was hunting on Farmers Loop when he saw a moose in a garden. He went up to the house and knocked on the door. A woman answered and he asked her if it would be all right if he shot the moose.

She said, "Sure, go ahead and shoot it."

He shot it, then the woman said. "Now get off my property. My husband has been hunting for two weeks and hasn't shot a thing."

The hunter was forced to walk off the property, leaving the moose for the woman and her husband.

HARRY'S TOLLGATE PLANS FALL THROUGH

*H*arry Underwood lived in a three-sided log house that was located near the large communication dishes behind the Refinery Lounge. He was one of the local characters. Some of his running mates were Jim Bradley, Jack Gustafson, Jack Parks, Frenchy Beuchane, and Maurice Laurence to name a few.

Harry's modern cabin was equipped with a pitcher pump and a well-traveled path to the outhouse. He later sold his place to Herb Dahl. He and his mother started a greenhouse business and later had a feedstore. The feedstore building is the boarded-up building just south of the Refinery Lounge. I might add, in passing, that Harry Underwood's nickname was Harry Underwear. In territorial days, the BLM (Bureau of Land Management) would hold drawings for parcels of land in many parts of the territory. They advertised for one drawing to be held for a group of five-acre recreation sites. These sites were to be sold for a set price to the winners of the drawing, and were located in the Harding Lake area.

Harry was one of the lucky winners. He hired a surveyor to identify his property so he could build a cabin on it. When the four corners had been established, he found that he owned a section of the Richardson Highway. If he built a cabin, it would be in the middle of the blacktop highway to the lower forty-eight.

He was somewhat irritated by this turn of events until he thought about the advantages of the situation. If he owned the highway, he could charge for crossing his property. He notified the *Fairbanks Daily News Miner* of his intent to install a tollgate on his property and make a fortune. Harry had a lot of fun with this situation and got a lot of mileage out of the press for three or four weeks. He never really intended to follow through with his threat to install the tollgate.

NIGHTCAP PROVES COSTLY FOR TRUCK

A few days ago, Orlo Holder called to tell me that he had a funny story for my column but he would not tell me over the phone. I went to his house for a visit, and in the course of a couple of hours received enough new, old-time stories to last a couple of months.

Orlo lives at 1/4 mile Plack Road, on a piece of property he obtained from Elmer Henry. Elmer worked with Orlo as a cement finisher. They had been friends and worked together for a number of years.

Plack Road had not been built at the time that Elmer built his house. He had to follow the slough upstream to cross over Badger Road, which is now the Wright Airway subdivision crossing. There was an old logging trail that went by his house and continued north for a mile or so. Elmer built a triangle drag out of 4x4 timbers with spikes driven through them on about six-inch centers. In the summer the road would get rutted, so he would tie this drag behind his car, pull it down to the crossing, and unhook it. When he came home from work, he would hook it on and drag it home.

One day he had his car worked on, so he asked Orlo to come get him and take him to work. Coming home from work the next night he had forgotten that Orlo had been to his house. He noticed a strange set of tire tracks and thought that someone was stealing from him.

The next morning he tied onto his drag and pulled it down to the crossing. He unhooked it, turned it upside down in his road, and went to work.

The next day he didn't show up for work on time. He did show up a couple hours later and explained to Orlo how he found out who had been stealing from him. He himself was the culprit. On his way home the night before, he had stopped at Blackie's Bar and had stayed too long. He started home and forgot about placing the drag in the middle of his road and ran over it. He was late for work because he had to buy three new tires before he could come in.

BEER IN OUTHOUSE OFFERS WORKER RESPITE

*T*hirty-five years ago Lew Dischner was business manager for the Carpenter's Local No. 1243 in Fairbanks. Later he was appointed as Commissioner of Labor by Governor Bill Egan, and moved to Juneau as a lobbyist. He became very successful at that until the Prudhoe Bay-to-Valdez pipeline was built. Then he became famous, or maybe infamous, for some dealings with the North Slope Borough that went sour. Thirty-five years ago, however, he was my friend and I visited him on several occasions when I happened to be in Juneau.

When I first knew Lew, he lived on Park Way in the Highway Park Subdivision, which was a part of the old Finnel homestead, in what is now part of the city of North Pole. One Saturday morning I stopped by his place to ask him to send me a carpenter for a couple of days to help me finish my house. He was in the process of building an apartment house on one of his lots. (It is still there). As I drove up, Lew was in the front yard and had a crew of men working. I saw that one of them was Eddie Morazus. He was a plumber friend of mine working out of Plumbers and Fitters Local No. 375. He was also Lew's brother-in-law and Lew had him scabbing in the plumbing for him.

While I was talking to Lew for a half an hour or so, we noticed that Eddie was rushing out to an outhouse that had been placed on the corner of the lot for use by the workers. He made several of those rush trips, so I said, "Lew, what is wrong with Eddie? Is he sick?"

Lew answered, "No, he isn't sick, there is nothing wrong with him. He doesn't want his wife to know that he's drinking. He has a six-pack of beer stashed in the outhouse."

TRAVELING HIGH SEAS IN 50'S MADE FOR GOOD CONVERSATION

*I*n the Fall of 1955 we were lucky enough to get a "space available outside" on the old *Funston,* a military ship which went from Whittier, Alaska to Seattle.

We caught the train in Fairbanks one night, and fourteen hours later were in Anchorage. We spent the night as guests of the air force at Elmendorf. The next morning we boarded the train again for Whittier and the *Funston.* That ship was one of two that made the trip to Alaska twice a month transporting troops. On this voyage we went to Kodiak. We spent the night and picked up troops from the coast guard and navy. It took the government several more years to figure out that it was cheaper to fly their personnel to duty stations than to house and feed them on surface transportation.

We had no problem with seasickness, but the report from the crowded decks below was that the enlisted people were sick for most of the trip. The seas were very rough when we hit the Japanese current after leaving Kodiak. On the upper deck, however, it was a most enjoyable trip.

Traveling with us were Major Woofter and his wife. He had been a master sergeant before World War II in charge of the Alaska communications system for the Signal Corps in Fairbanks. He told me he had been on the keyboard in Fairbanks the night of April 14, 1912, when Alaska received the news of the sinking of the Titanic.

When we boarded the ship it was the last time we saw his wife until we reached Seattle.

Major Woofter and I had several good visits during that trip. He had received a direct commission during World War II and retired as a major after thirty-five years. We were assigned a table in the mess hall and for each meal we were with the same people. Our tablemates consisted of a staff sergeant, his lovely blonde wife, and a warrant officer who had served more than twenty-five years in the military. He was on his way to the states to retire.

At the first meal we introduced ourselves and got acquainted. The pretty blonde asked the warrant officer what his plans were, adding that he didn't look old enough to retire.

He said, "I'm a lot older than I look. I was water boy for Gen. Custer."

"Yes, but that doesn't count towards today's retirement," she replied.

INJURED RUSSIAN TEENS GET PRIORTY MERCY FLIGHT

*O*n April 11th, 1992, I caught a flight from Eielson Air Force Base on an air evacuation plane to Norton Air Force Base in Anchorage. We were told the morning of April 12th that the flight from Elmendorf to Norton would be delayed because they were waiting for a plane to land with more patients. We finally boarded the C-141 aircraft and were told to sit tight and wait for a Lear jet to land with two Russian burn patients aboard. The mission would be rerouted from McChord Air Force Base in Tacoma, Washington, to Kelly Air Force Base in San Antonio, Texas.

The Lear jet landed at 11:45 A.M., loaded two patients aboard and we took off from Elmendorf on a mission. The flight crew said that the flight had been arranged by the state department as a humanitarian act. The patients were two teenage boys, age thirteen and fifteen who lived in Moscow. They had been playing with gasoline and matches and were burned over sixty-five percent of their bodies. They were reported to be in serious, but stable condition. The Lear jet was from Life Line, which had been contracted to do this service through Providence Hospital in Anchorage. I was told that Life Line waived their fee for the flight which was from Anchorage to Moscow and back again.

We were never told who the boys were or how the accident happened or exactly how the flight came about. They were accompanied by Dr. Hasselquist from Elmendorf and an English speaking Russian doctor who had a name no one could pronounce.

We landed at McChord Air Force Base and off-loaded twenty-eight passengers who were patients for Madigan Army Hospital at Tacoma, Washington, and then continued the flight to Kelly Air Force Base in San Antonio, Texas. There, the two boys were transported to Brooks Army Medical Center.

A couple of hours later we continued our flight to Norton, arriving in San Bernadino at 3:30 A.M. Since no one could pronounce the doctor's name, I took it upon myself to get his signature on my notebook. I snagged him as he walked to the back of the plane. I got his autograph and he wrote on my notebook, "My name is Sezgey."

EARLY YEARS OF EIELSON AREA GRANGE

I was asked by the Eielson Area Grange to do a story on the Grange's early years, so here it is.

Don McKee and his wife Alice organized the Eielson Area Grange No. 6 at the VFW Hall. Leo Morris was elected the first master. The grange met for a couple of years in the VFW Hall until they managed to lease four or five acres along the slough where the grange hall is at this time. The new hall was dedicated on July 27, 1968, by William B. Pearson of the National Grange.

As deputy state master of Alaska granges, here is my report as given in 1970 at the 104th annual session in Boise, Idaho:

"Greetings from the Alaska State Grange Council to the 104th annual session. The year 1970 has been a busy one for Alaska's Grangers. The Two Rivers Grange elected a live-wire Master, and have this year doubled their membership. They invited the State Grange Council to hold its annual meeting in their newly finished log Grange Hall to help celebrate their tenth anniversary. As part of this meeting they had an old-fashioned fair with booths and games. All of the subordinate Granges show an increase in membership for this year except for our Junior Grange. The membership growth is not as much as it should have been, but we do show a thirty-five percent gain for 1970.

While the Alaska legislature was in session this spring, I was asked to attend the session along with the president of the Cattlemen's Association, a representative of the grain farmers, and two produce farmers to try and get an appropriation for the Alaska Farmers Revolving Loan Fund. We met with the Resource Committee for the House and with the Finance Committee for the Senate and came out with one million dollars—five hundred thousand for emergency irrigation and five hundred thousand for the general loan fund.

There are six of us attending this convention from Alaska. May I

100

present: Sister Grace Morris, State Grange Council, Secretary and Treasurer; Brother Leo Morris, past Subordinate and Pomona Master; Sister Ray Mullin, State Grange Woman's Act Chairman the Alta Peck of Alaska; Brother Gary Mullin, Eielson Area Grange first Lecturer; Sister, and my wife, Gerry Lewis, past State Grange Secretary, Treasurer. Fraternally submitted, William G. Lewis."

At a baby shower at the Grange Hall for a young married couple, we were all gathered around the bassinet looking down on the infant. Leo Morris looked at the child and said, "It looks exactly like Bill Lewis." The startled mother said, "I didn't even know Bill Lewis at that time."

WHY I STOPPED WRITING FOR THE FAIRBANKS DAILY NEWS MINER

When you write a column for a newspaper, you sometimes write one that someone is unhappy with. In May of 1992, one of my little stories made a friend of mine so mad he threatened to sue the *News Miner,* me, and anyone connected with us. It resulted in me getting fired from my well-paid one-hundred-dollar-a-month job. Here is the story as printed, only the name has been changed. I have changed the name in order to protect the guilty. It is the only name that has been changed in this book.

Several years ago while working on one of the Nike sites the union sent out an apprentice. It was his first job as he was still in high school, but he was to work during his summer vacation.

He was assigned to me as my working partner. His name was I.P. Freely. He had been told that he could not be a journeyman unless he finished high school. He was not doing well in his studies in school and when asked what was giving him problems he said he just couldn't get interested in his schoolwork, had to repeat his junior year, and was not doing well in his senior year.

When I asked him which subjects were giving him the most trouble he said, "All of them." In order to get some idea as to what they were teaching at that time I began to question him about what seemed to be important to his teachers at the time. I remembered what seemed important to my teachers back in 1928 to 1932 so I asked him a series of questions.

"Who invented the steamboat?" He answered, "I don't know." I said, "Robert Fulton."

"Who invented the incandescent light bulb?" His answer, "I don't know." I said, "Thomas Edison."

"Who invented the cotton gin?" Answer: "I don't know." I said, "Eli Whitney."

"Who invented the telephone?" Answer: "I don't know." I said, "Alexandar Graham Bell."

Then he started to complain that these were not fair questions, so I told him that in my time everyone had to learn these things.

To prove it, Bill Anderson, who was of my generation, walked by where we were working. I asked him who was the first man to fly solo across the Atlantic. Without hesitation he said, "Charles Lindbergh."

I.P. said that none of these questions were fair and he shouldn't be expected to know them. I asked him why they were unfair questions and he replied, "They aren't fair to me because you guys were here when all that happened."

After the story caused so much trouble and Editor Dan Joling fired me, I wrote an apology to be printed in the *Fairbanks Daily News Miner* but Publisher Paul Massey refused to print it and advised me to let sleeping dogs lie. I would have never thought of calling I.P. a sleeping dog. A lot of people have asked why my column was discontinued. Now you know.

A humorous collection of stories written by Bill Lewis who has lived in the vicinity of North Pole Alaska for forty years. He came to Alaska as a retired Air Force Officer and worked as a journeyman plumber out of Local 375 for enough years to retire and worked for the State of Alaska long enough to retire as Alaska Director of Agriculture. He says if you don't think this book is funny he will gladly give you your money back; if he hasn't already spent it!